HOW

TO BE A

FINANCIALLY

SUCCESSFUL

CHRISTIAN

BY

Sam O. Oluwafemi

How to be a
Financially Successful Christian
..Seed time and harvest shall not cease, the word of God is settled, is our application of the principles settled?

ISBN: 978 - 978 – 58327 – 4 - 7

Published by:
D. GLORY OF GOD ENTERPRISES
30, Olorunkemi Street, Off Joju Road Araromi Quarters, Sango ota, Ogun State.
Tel: 08099712477, 09047017714
E-mail: d.gogtechnology@gmail.com, d.gogenterprises@yahoo.com

Table of Contents

A DIFFERENCE

God said; I will put a difference between the Egyptians and the Israelites - **Exodus 11 v 7**. This means there must be a difference between the believer in Christ and the unbeliever. What tangible difference do we have between the believers and the unbelievers today in terms of finance? I leave you to answer that.

Why are we suffering like the unbeliever, going through the same things they are going through? Simply because we are living our Christian lives based on the fore-knowledge we have before we came into Christ. We are doing God's things our ways not God's ways, no one is exempted, except, the person is tried and not found wanting.

Lack of knowledge, lack of application and lack of accurate application.

Let us learn how to do God's things God's way then shall we experience what God says we would experience.

INTRODUCTION
FOUR WAYS OF SUCCESS

There are four major known ways of being successful in life, they are;

- **Natural ways**
- **Educational or Intellectual ways**
- **Devil's ways**
- **God's ways**

Natural ways: The natural ways of being successful is to take life as it comes, you are successful if you are born in a successful home, destined to be successful, receive help somehow that turn things around, favoured by season or nature etc. As long as it is not something you specially made arrangement for but it happened somehow and made you successful is natural. You can pray to God for this, he may help.

Educational and Intellectual: Quality education or being educated in a good area of specialization or business can help someone to be financially successful. So also if you are wise and intellectual; I mean being wise in the affairs of the system of this world, this is one of the route for many young people. Use your brain to enrich yourself, it does matter who get hurt, it's a game of manipulation and of the survivor of the fittest.

Devil's ways: The devil's way involves ritual of different kinds. This is dealing directly with the devil; he demands some certain sacrifices and gives laws and principles. The devil makes his devotees financially successful by connecting them with others that are his own who have gain grounds, this give them access to contracts, businesses, loans and opportunities and to some he gives power to invoke money, power to collect or divert money, businesses, contracts, position that is not supposed to come to them. Even though there is a terrible ending for this, many still go into it with their minds made up to enjoy the pleasure for a season.

God's way: God's ways of being successful involves applying God's given principles of finance. This is not about prayer except in some certain areas where it is applicable. This is majorly doing what God's says to do that has to do with finance. If these principles of finance are applied as they should be, the financial blessing they carry will be experienced by the person that is practicing them. You do it, you get it, you don't do it, you don't get it.

In this book, our discussion is totally based on God's ways of accumulating riches. I am aware this is not the only means. Everybody is not rich and successful through God's ways, if you desire to be financially successful through God's ways, then you need to consider the things we are about to discuss and put them to work, they are difficult to practice which is why many look for easier alternatives, but they are the only ways you can accumulate durable riches and wealth that have no sorrows. All other means of riches have sorrows, choose wisely.

Proverbs 10 v 22

> ***10:22 The blessing of the LORD, it maketh rich, and he addeth no sorrow with it.***

It is God's desire for us to prosper financially, not just to prosper but to have durable riches without sorrows, to make it possible for us to enjoy the blessing that makes rich and add no sorrow, He laid down certain financial principles to be enforced by His Ministers that we can apply to our Christian walk which will produce effective financial results. But what do we see today? It is as though God laid down these financial principles so as to enrich Ministers but according to God's plan, the aim is to enrich the members, majority of God's children are tired of tithing in particular because the result is not vivid as declared by God. My question is; why is it that we don't get the result God says we will receive after applying any of the principles? I believe there is a fault somewhere; we have to look into where the fault is coming from. God's word is settled, it always works, this makes God blameless but the remaining factors involve are not blameless until they are all tried. The remaining factors includes; the member; his walk with God, his seed, offering and tithes, the Minister and the Ministry. My dear brother, don't be tired of these principles, find out who or what is at fault and then apply the proper solution. If we cannot get these principles to work for us, we wouldn't be able to live above low natural life and its frustrations. I cannot afford to go about my finance the world way, as much as I desire to be successful; it must be through the principles of God's financial riches that brings God's blessing and add no sorrows.

If this is your decision also, then let us carefully pay a keen attention to what we need to do.

God bless you.

Note: I am a fellow church member, a brother just like you; I pay my tithes, I pay my offerings and seeds. I had to seek for answers when I wasn't getting the results the word of God says I was supposed to get after applying the laid down God's financial principles. Listen to me as a fellow brother as I share these with you and know for sure that I am for you not against you.

HOW TO BE A FINANCIALLY SUCCESSFUL CHRISTIAN

In this book will find out

- If God want us to be rich financially.
- Then we will also find out if anybody can be financially rich.
- God's principle of being rich
- How to apply these principles
- Importance of the principles
- Results of each principle
- How to keep growing financially
- How to maintain riches
- Final remarks

DOES GOD WANTS US FINANCIALLY RICH?

It is very important for us to find out if God is in support or want us to be financially rich. Knowing this will help us to know God's mind concerning our financial life. Any strong argument must start from Genesis. We will have to see God's original plan and structure for man then we can proceed to any other writings of the scripture.

1st book of genesis, lets read from the 27th verse to 28;

1:27 ***So God created man in his own image, in the image of God created he him; male and female created he them.***

1:28 ***And God blessed them, and God said unto them, Be fruitful, and multiply, and replenish the earth, and subdue it: and have*** *dominion over the fish of the sea, and over the fowl of the air, and over every living thing that moveth upon the earth.*

When you read downward, you will see that man was created for enjoyment.

Somebody may say; no financially riches in there. Oops! You are missing it, relax!

Firstly, Man was made to enjoy his life that is what I want you to see first. We both know without money, enjoyment is not complete.

Secondly, man was created to have dominion. Why do you think your Boss at work can control you at will and call on you whenever he wants? It's because he has dominion over you, how did he get it? Money gave it to him. So there is money inside that verse.

To be a strong man/woman money is involve. Whether you believe it or not, it doesn't change anything. I believe you know when you have good money in your pocket or account, the way you talk and act will be different. From what we see in Genesis, we both know if you want to have dominion, power, influence, you must have money.

Let see that Genesis 1 v 27-29 in this form. God said; *"I have given you every herb bearing seeds, I have*

given you dominion over the fish, fowl, and everything that creepeth upon the earth"

Tell me, which of these things mentioned above can you have today without money? Is it land to build or plant on, tree (plank to roof your house), vegetable to cook your soup, meat to put inside your soup or fruits that you eat? Tell me, which of these can you get without money? So I'll say, open your heart and not your head. What I actually wanted you to see there is that God created man to have a good life, to enjoy that life today, money is involved.

Let's see if Jesus wants us to have money. Hahaha-I am enjoying this. God is just so wonderful, as I am writing this book now, the anointing of the Holy Spirit is just all about money and I am seeing money in every single chapter and verse of the Bible. If anyone will speed read the words of the Master, it's very easy to say that Jesus don't care about us having money, which is not true. He cares about us having money more than you could ever desire to have. You may ask ***"are you saying Jesus too wants me to have money more than I actually want to have?"*** I am saying yes; **all the cars, beautiful houses, happy homes, helping people financially, giving huge amounts for Church projects**? Yes

Jesus wants even more for you and me. Lack of understanding makes people take the little things out of the hand of God and leave the big ones to fall to the ground. The scripture I am about to read, if you are not patience enough, you will be picking the same thing many have picked out of it, leaving the biggest of them. Now; watch and be calm, okay? This money matter is a very sensitive matter in the kingdom of God. The writing I about to show you is an account of a conversation of Jesus and a rich ruler who wanted to justify himself. Jesus made a statement here that has been misunderstood everywhere. This man was asking Jesus what he must do to inherit eternal life.

St Luke 18 what I want you to see is the answer of Jesus to the man from the twenty-second verse.

Luke 18 v 22 – 25

> *18:22 Now when Jesus heard these things, he said unto him, Yet lackest thou one thing: sell all that thou hast, and distribute unto the poor, and thou shalt have treasure in heaven: and come, follow me.*
>
> *18:23 And when he heard this, he was very sorrowful: for he was very rich.*

18:24 And when Jesus saw that he was very sorrowful, he said, HOW HARDLY SHALL THEY THAT HAVE RICHES ENTER INTO THE KINGDOM OF GOD!

18:25 For it is easier for a camel to go through a needle's eye, THAN FOR A RICH MAN TO ENTER INTO THE KINGDOM OF GOD.

Hey! Don't bite me yet. I know that scripture too and I am seeing what you are seeing. Now let me show you what I am seeing because you are not seeing what I am seeing.

My goodness! Follow me carefully.

The argumentative word there is **"How hardly shall they that have riches enter into the kingdom of God".** Before I show you this, I want you to know that there is difference between a man that read the Bible and a man that study the word of God. I am a man who received instruction to study so as to show myself approved to God, a workman who needs not to be ashamed of his profession, rightly dividing the word of truth. So I'll say, don't get offended, but hear me out; People who receives instruction as I did, always comes up with words out of the mouth of God which can be offensive to those that read the Bible. There is something called ***"motive behind a***

statement", a statement may have a particular meaning, but the original motive behind the statement may be different from the meaning. This is one of the reasons God looks at the hearts (motive behind every action) than the sounding of the statement.

NOTE: When you find a strange argument in the Bible, always search out the matter. Do not also forget that there is limitation in the translations of all the accounts.

Now the account we read in Luke 18 picking out **22nd to 25th** we can also see the same record **Mark 10 v 17-13**, our reading will be the **24th verse**

Mark 10 v 24

> ***10:24 And the disciples were astonished at his words. But Jesus answereth again, and saith unto them, Children, how hard is it for THEM THAT TRUST in riches to enter into the kingdom of God!***

You see that? It not about being rich, it's about trusting in your riches instead of trusting God. As it is written; curse is the man that put his trust in man (riches). Don't forget riches are a strong city, a strong hold, so it's easy to put trust in riches. Jesus was not emphasizing that is bad to be rich or have problem with anyone that is having riches, but there is a big problem if anyone put his trust in riches, and turn his riches to his god. Jesus said you cannot serve mammon and serve God at the same time; meaning, you cannot make your riches your god and still make Jehovah your God. I think that is clear enough. The motive behind the statement is clear now.

Let's now progress to our original subject. Jesus wants us to have riches but it has to be based on the kingdom's principle. To clarify this, the disciples were also concerned as you and I are concerned now. They were surprised when Jesus made that statement. Jesus made it clear that those that trust in their riches are the ones that will find it hard to enter the Kingdom of God. To show that Jesus wants riches for us, He said in the 29th – 30th verse of same Mark 10,

10:29 ***And Jesus answered and said, Verily I say unto you, There is no man that hath left house, or brethren, or sisters, or father, or mother, or wife, or children, or lands, for my sake, and the gospel's,***

10:30 ***But he shall receive an hundredfold now in***

this time, houses, and brethren, and sisters, and mothers, and children, and lands, with persecutions; and in the world to come eternal life.

Luke 18 vs 29 and **Mathew 19 vs 27-30**, we will receive whatever we forsake to follow him (The rich man would have receive a hundred fold of all his riches if he had followed Jesus). If you don't have detail study on this also, you will miss it again by thinking Jesus is saying that we will receive an hundred fold in heaven or after resurrection. Let's us now see if the reward is right here on earth or if it is after resurrection.

Mathew 19 vs 29.

19:29 And every one that hath forsaken houses, or brethren, or sisters, or father, or mother, or wife, or children, or lands, for my name's sake, shall receive an hundredfold, and shall inherit everlasting life.

If you read this scripture in Mathew alone you will not have a full light concerning this, the Lord was actually saying that we will receive this on earth so that we can be rich enough to help the poor and needy and the hope of big reward in heaven will still be there. If you have the mentality that he is talking about when we get to Heaven, you will suffer on earth till you die, and your sufferings will not bring you reward but shame, because you frustrated the grace of God and announced to the world and all creation that God is wicked and his Son's death brought you poverty .

Now let's read the same story in Mark and Luke.
Open your Bible please! Mark 10 v 29-30

10:29 ***And Jesus answered and said, Verily I say unto you, There is no man that hath left house, or brethren, or sisters, or father, or mother, or wife, or children, or lands, for my sake, and the gospel's,***

10:30 ***But he shall receive an hundredfold NOW IN THIS TIME, houses, and brethren, and sisters, and mothers, and children, and lands, with persecutions; and in the world to come eternal life.***

Did you see the differences? The persecution here is not suffering of poverty; it's about people who will say all many of words against you because you preach Christ or because of your possessions.
It is written in the word that at the mouth of two witnesses, a matter is established. Even if there are

no two witnesses concerning this, I would still prove to you that Mark is more accurate on this subject.

Firstly, in Heaven, there is no buying of lands and houses. Jesus said in my father house there are many mansions, He has prepared a place for us, and there is a statement there that indicates it will happen here on earth before our forever living in the world to come; ***"Now in this time"***.

Let's see Luke's written concerning this

Luke 18 vs 29

18:29 And he said unto them, Verily I say unto you, There is no man that hath left house, or parents, or brethren, or wife, or children, for the kingdom of God's sake,

18:30 Who shall not receive manifold more IN THIS PRESENT TIME, and in the world to come life everlasting.

You see it now? So it's good to study the word and not just speed read the Bible.

What Jesus is saying here directly is, if you follow me and forsake yourself that is; deny yourself of the earthly pleasures, leaving your normal life just because of me, he says; you will receive one hundred fold of everything here on earth.

In conclusion Jesus wants us wealthy, by the time you receive hundred fold of the things he mentioned, have you not become wealthy? Think about lands alone. Let's assume you are to receive one hundred plots of land presently (**2016**), by the time you sell or lease it out, that will give you huge amount of money right? I told you in the entire word I am seeing money - hahahahaha!

In most places around Lagos now one plot of land is worth more than a million naira (2016). So if you have one hundred plots of land and you sell it, you will be worth one hundred million naira or more. Will you have one hundred million naira (July 2016) or one hundred million dollars and still say you are not rich? I told you money is everywhere in the word of God.

So Jesus wants us to be rich and wealthy. Come to think of it; if the children of the Most High God are to be poor, then who did God made the beautiful things in this world for? For Lucifer his enemy or his children who continually provoke the anger of the Merciful God with their wickedness? No way. Say this with me; **"The best in this world belongs to me".**

Right now, I open your understanding in the name of Jesus Christ, Be opened!

Name one President in the world whose children are suffering, even the local government chairman's children are known for their extravagant and luxurious spending. How much more they that are heirs of the promise made to faithful Abraham.

Wake-up and possess your possession. The preachers that got familiar with "**money is the root of all evil**" forgot that the scripture did not say money is the root of all evil but "**the love of money".**

They never asked how come Solomon did not throw his money away. Till now there is still no King, President, Emperor or any ruler who is as wealthy as Solomon was, God blessed King Solomon, blessed Papa Abraham, Blessed King David. Picking up isolated scriptures to condemn a good thing is dangerous.

Let us have a look at the scripture.

1Timothy 6 v 10

> ***6:10 FOR THE LOVE OF MONEY is the root of all evil: which while some coveted after, they have erred from the faith, and pierced themselves through with many sorrows.***

Money is not the root of all evil, but the love of it. Out of the heart proceeds evil not out of money;

Matthew 15 v 18 – 19

15:18 But those things which proceed out of the mouth come forth from the heart; and they defile the man.

15:19 For out of the heart proceed evil thoughts, murders, adulteries, fornications, thefts, false witness, blasphemies:

With these it is clear that it is the heart of man that is desperately wicked that makes men do wicked things with money or because of money, so it is not the money but the man.

Jeremiah 17 v 9

17:9 The heart is deceitful above all things, and desperately wicked: who can know it?

"It is not the gun that kills; it is the one that fires it". There is no scripture that says money is evil or money is devilish. Money is good. Come to think of it, if money is not needed then Jesus wouldn't say "**Go into all the world**", did he not know we will need transportations, either by road or air, is he not aware that the hungry need to be fed? Or has he forgotten we are no longer in the wilderness where we wake up in the morning and collect manner?

C'mon, Jesus is not naïve or short of sight that he doesn't know tomorrow.

Let's see what the Apostles said about of finances. One day, Apostle Paul was talking to certain Christians; he told them that it is necessary for the saints to partake in their material blessing as the Christians are partakers of the Minister's spiritual blessings.

1Corinthians 9 v 11

9:11 ***If we have sown unto you spiritual things, is it a great thing if we shall reap your carnal things?***

God wants it so, since God want it so, then He also has to make provision for the Christians so that they will have more than enough to sustain the ministers and other financial needs. Since there is always a financial need in the house of God and Ministry, it is clear that God has to make his children rich so that his work will be done and to avoid His name being blasphemed among the heathens.

If God is against his children being rich, there will be no financial need in the church. Many Believers don't understand that one of the reasons God has to bless us by all means is for us to use it in executing

His Business, do his work and to live His life that he has given to us. Before God places a demand, he would have made provision for it.

"What God would demand God would provide" - T. D Jakes

We see this happening over and over again. God will not ask you for what he did not give you; that will be an act of wickedness. Before the instruction to Cain and Abel's sacrifice, there was Ram and Yam, before God destroyed mankind with water saving Noah and his family there was a big ark, before Adam sinned against God there was an instruction, before God asked Abraham for Isaac as sacrifice He gave him Isaac. Before God says give me, He has made provision for it. This is why no man takes the glory in the things of God by saying "**I did**" it's always "**God did it**" because we have come to know, it's ***"Him that works in us both to will and to do of His good pleasure"***. The thought to do it, the ability to start it, the strength to keep you going, the power to finish it, It's all God's, for these course we Glory not in our works but in the finished works of Jesus Christ.

Apostle John says;

3 John 1 v 2

1:2 ***Beloved, I wish above all things that thou mayest prosper and be in health, even as thy soul prospereth.***

The "**prosper**" here is not in spiritual things it's in material things - I mean in finances. It's so because Apostle John uttered this statement while complimenting the financial good deeds by the Church.

From this stand point it is clear that God, Jesus and the Apostles wants us rich so that we can further the Gospel. Our place of worship should be good; we should be able to help others. These are some of the responsibilities committed to us. Many don't believe a Christian is suppose be full of money because they don't understand what we are called to do. I still don't understand how anyone can preach the gospel effectively round the world even in his own city effectively for Jesus to come without money. It's either Jesus did not mean what he said or the believers who think such don't understand what it means to preach round the whole world. When you catch this vision you will understand that the reason there is money on earth is for you to use it to preach the gospel. Do you know that it's only the children (sons and daughters) of God that actually knows the value of money, how to spend money and what to spend money on? When you know this, you will understand that the reason governments are printing money everywhere in the world is because of you.

The natural man spends money on cars, houses, drinks, smoke, sickness, food, children, wives (women), to rule over the poor and to oppress them. That's all they know. Believers spend money on: furthering the gospel, helping others, putting smiles on people's face with money and the word of God, making his knowledge available.

Which of these is doing God's service? If you were God, who will you give more? The one caring for himself and his family alone? Or the one doing good to others which is actually God's work? Make the decision. Life is sweet and beautiful; it's all a matter of choice.

If you are still having some doubt or not fully persuaded that God, Jesus and the Apostles want us rich then I'll say you should show me men who whole heartedly walked with God and were poor. I mean lack money. Papa A.B (Abraham) was so blessed that the people that were on the land feared him; same thing with Isaac, Jacob was of no difference, read his story. He went to Laban's house with his clothes alone he returned to his father's land with great riches including servants.

According to the scriptures, in Christ Jesus, we are made partakers of the same blessing. Who do you want to resemble? Choose your role model. As for me and my house we have chosen Abraham in riches as a role model and in faith. It is written that we should look up to Abraham so I am looking at Abraham and his lifestyle, all I see is blessings, riches, greatness, friendship with God, faith that shakes heaven and move the earth.

I'll leave you here with clarification on this; don't forget those who have problem with riches in the kingdom of God (Church) are always referred to as church rats. I am doing all I can to get your spirit fully established in this matter, that you may accept it and embrace it. If you cannot accept that God, Jesus and the Apostles wants you rich, the rest of this book will not be effective neither will you produce result with it. What a man cannot believe he cannot have. Believe and see a transformation in your financial status.

Let's move to the next aspect which is: who can be rich as a Christian.

2

WHO CAN BE FINANCIALLY RICH?

This is a very interesting question. This question is the same as asking who can receive Abrahamic blessings. We cannot talk about riches without bringing Abraham in. He is the genesis of the blessings of a believer in Christ Jesus. Anyone who believes that Jesus is the son of God; He came to die for his/her sins and was raised for his/her justification, this is he who comes with blood and water. This man/woman is accounted a joint hair with Christ Jesus, being a joint heir he is automatically qualified to be a partaker of the blessings God gave to Abraham. This man has license to be rich the same way Abraham was rich even richer.

Here is an opportunity, if you have not make Jesus the Lord of your life whole heartedly, do so now calling upon the Son of the living God to come into your life so as to wash you from your sins, and be a partaker of these blessings.

If you have been playing with your Christianity, it's time to stop the messing around and be serious with your salvation by rededicating your life to Jesus Christ by acknowledging your instability in the faith with fasting and prayers.

Anybody in Christ Jesus has been made rich already.

2Corinthians 8 v 9

8:9 For ye know the grace of our Lord Jesus Christ, that, though he was rich, yet for your sakes he became poor, that ye through his poverty might be rich.

All you need is to find out what you need to do to manifest the riches that are already deposited in your spiritual account, that is; how to withdraw your spiritual money to your physical account - all the money you could ever need has been deposited in your spiritual account the day you whole heartedly made Jesus the Lord of your life. Jesus was made poor that through his poverty, you and I might be rich, and through Jesus Christ we have access to all the treasures of God.

In conclusion anyone in Christ that believes is part of Abraham's blessing therefore such a one can be a financially successful Christian. You must believe it!

Because all things are possible for him that believes; after believing, you must act it out, that is talk big, see yourself big, and think big. You may say: But I don't have much now. Well that is why this book is for you, that is exactly why you are reading it, I so much believe if you already have so much to the full, you wouldn't care to buy this book neither will you ready it even if it is given to you for free.

"They that are whole need no physician"

"Jesus Christ did not come to save that which is saved but that which is lost"

"Jesus Christ did not come for people that are already righteous but for sinners to be made righteous"

"Jesus Christ has not come to make the rich and wealthy richer and wealthier but to call the poor to inherit a blessing and become rich, wealthy and successful"

The essence of studying this book is to learn something that can elevate your financial situation and that is exactly the aim of the book.

Since we are talking about Abraham blessings, we must also talk about AB's faith, so that we may act the same way he acted, that is what role model is all about, find out what the person did, and do the same.

Before Abraham had a son he was called Abram, meaning, *"**Assumed Father**"*, God renamed him Abraham, ***"Father of Many"***. Did he have many children then, No, not even one. Abraham announced to everyone that he is the father of many. So, you keep telling everyone around you that you have money everywhere, that actually, you are number one in the list of the richest peoples in the world; if anyone says it's not true that they have the list and your name is not there, tell them you just got promoted and that list they are holding is an outdated one. As soon as the record is updated they will see your name. If they keep pressing, then use the Bible to explain to them that **"all things are mine"**, I have everything.

1Corinthians 3 v 21 – 23

3:21 Therefore let no man glory in men. FOR ALL THINGS ARE YOURS;

3:22 Whether Paul, or Apollos, or Cephas, or the world, or life, or death, or things present, or things to come; all are yours;

3:23 And ye are Christ's; and Christ is God's.

It sounds crazy right? But that is faith. That's exactly how crazy papa AB's sounded in the presence of his savants and everyone around him, calling him crazy old man who still have no son at old age and yet claiming to be father of many. Did he not get the son? Yes! Did he become father of many? Yes! Since he becomes father of many, then whatever it is you have been saying you are, you are and you shall be, and whatever you have been claiming you have, you shall have, just make sure you are at it, putting the right principles in place.

You have done the outer part of it. As you are talking to people about what God says, you have align your thoughts in that direction also, thinking about it and then use your imagination to see yourself living that life of abundance. Why is this important? It is important because **"as a man thinks in his heart so is he".** You begin to think ownership no more rentage. Think of lending to people, no more borrowing. Think of power, money gives power, think of employing people, no more looking for job. Think of helping others, no more looking for help. Think of what you can do for God, no more looking for what God should do for you; let it become "**what can I do for God**?" Then start giving in your church with a willing heart according to your present ability (do not frustrate yourself by trying to do what your ability cannot carry that will make you murmur and complain, God love a cheerful giver) and helping others and other churches to grow financially.

2Corinthians 9 v 7

> ***9:7 Every man according as he purposeth in his heart, so let him give; not grudgingly, or of necessity: for God loveth a cheerful giver.***

Think sponsoring people both in church and around you. Think global not local.

When you begin to think like this, your words will be aligned in this direction which will cause you to walk in what you have been thinking about, in other words; you will become what you have been thinking about eventually, actually, what you are now, is the result of what you have been thinking about yourself to be, think something better, you shall be better. God will begin to show you how your thoughts can be accomplished.

"As a man thinketh in his heart, so is he" - Proverbs 23 v 7.

After thinking, taking actions with steps is next. Think what you can do and start with what you have. If it's giving in church, start with what you have available. If it's helping others, start with what you have, if it's spreading the Gospel, God will show you how to start or what to start with. Don't wait, start!

"The best time to start is by starting immediately after learning, hearing or reading".

Once these three things are in place, you are positioned for greatness. Don't forget to be giving thanks, glory and honor to the Lord in the midst of the thinking, talking and acting; and God will prosper you.

It is now clear that every child of God in Christ Jesus can be rich. Do you know that this is not supposed to be an argument? You don't really need explanation to believe this. If earthly things are still difficult to believe at this age of Christianity, how can we believe revelations and visions? Or even heavenly things? Step up!

Every parent desire their children to be rich, those who could not give their children quality life do hope their daughters get married to a rich man so that their daughters will not suffer, by this they will be able to help them too. As wicked and selfish we are, if we could desire good things for our own children, how much more our heavenly father.

Anyone, anywhere who professes that it is bad to be rich as a Christian, poverty will never depart out of his / her life because such a one has presented God of heaven and earth a wicked being therefore wickedness shall be his / her heritage.

My dear brothers and sisters, poverty is a curse as a result of sin. A Christian is no longer under any bondage of sin and curse because Jesus has paid for us.

Let's wake up and seize our inheritance. Let no one deprive you of your liberty and rights in Christ neither should you deprive yourself.

Since you now know and believe you can be rich, let's see God's principle concerning financial riches.

GOD'S PRINCIPLES ON FINANCIAL RICHES

God will not lay financial principles if He is against financial riches or if they are impossible. Of what use is a manual if there is no machine to use it on? Or of what importance is food if there is no stomach? God has laid down rules and regulations that govern riches, increase in riches and a life of abundance of riches. These principles worked then, they still work now, and they will work till Jesus comes. After Jesus' coming, if there will still be seed time and harvest time, the principles will still work.

Suffering is a result of doing things our ways and not God's ways. God has a plan for the riches of His kids, but most of God's children love to use the world system to get rich. In the world today, how rich you are or how rich you will be can be determined by the kind of business you run, your kind of Job, how smart you are, how educated you are, how greedy you are, the extent you can go so as to get money etc. all these are some of the ways of the natural man and woman to gather riches. None of these ways is compatible with the plans of God for His kids.

Let us see something from the scripture;

***Proverbs* 23 *v* 4**

23:4 *Labour not to be rich: cease from thine own wisdom.*

The rich King Solomon said this by the inspiration of the Spirit of God. This man was very rich, what he is saying here is that; he did not labour to be rich. Now if God is saying we should not labour to be rich, how do we get riches then? The children of men live their entire lives laboring day and night so as to heap up riches and the child of God is doing the same. Though this was one of the ways we knew before coming to Christ, now that we are in Christ, we ought to learn God's ways. It's high time we stop living in the Kingdom of God with our formal lives styles.

Do you know that sweating and laboring hard so as to earn a living is part of the curse of Adam?

If you have not studied you must be born again, please call us to order for it, it is free.

Genesis 3 v 17 – 19

3:17 *And unto Adam he said, Because thou hast hearkened unto the voice of thy wife, and hast eaten of the tree, of which I commanded thee, saying, Thou shalt not eat of it: cursed is the ground for thy sake; IN SORROW SHALT THOU EAT OF IT ALL THE DAYS OF THY LIFE;*

3:18 *Thorns also and thistles shall it bring forth to thee; and thou shalt eat the herb of the field;*

3:19 *IN THE SWEAT OF THY FACE SHALT THOU EAT BREAD, TILL THOU RETURN UNTO THE GROUND; for out of it wast thou taken: for dust thou art, and unto dust shalt thou return.*

Being in Christ has made it possible for us to have a life that this curse is not attached with, that is why we must be born again by water and Holy Ghost baptism which impart the life of God into us after confessing the lordship of Jesus Christ. We are no longer under the curse of Adam.

Romans 5 v 15 – 18

5:15 *But not as the offence, so also is the free gift. For if through the offence of one many be dead, much more the grace of God, and the gift by grace, which is by one man, Jesus Christ, hath abounded unto many.*

5:16 *And not as it was by one that sinned, so is the gift: for the judgment was by one to condemnation, but the free gift is of many offences unto justification.*

5:17 *For if by one man's offence death reigned by one; much more they which receive abundance of grace and of the gift of righteousness shall reign in life by one, Jesus Christ.)*

5:18 *Therefore as by the offence of one judgment came upon all men to condemnation; even so by the righteousness of one the free gift came upon all men unto justification of life.*

Moreover, it is written;

Proverbs 10 v 22

10:22 *The blessing of the LORD, it maketh rich, and he addeth no sorrow with it.*

With this; if whatever you do to earn money involves too much labour, wearing you out always and at the end whatever you make is not able to give you the kind of life you desire, it means that you are not enjoying the blessings of God that maketh rich and addeth no sorrow which could be as a result of you not reborn with the new life of God even though you go to church or you are not running your life according to the way God has instructed us to live.

Christians are suffering too much, it has almost become impossible to differentiate a Christian and none Christian in terms of financial blessing. Though as a Child of God, we are not to be surprised seeing the ungodly man heaping up rich or sweating day and night. God has given them the ability to labour, toil day and night to heap up riches.

Ecclesiastes 2 v 26

2:26 For God giveth to a man that is good in his sight wisdom, and knowledge, and joy: but to the sinner he giveth travail, to gather and to heap up, that he may give to him that is good before God. This also is vanity and vexation of spirit.

Travailing, laboring day and night is not the life style of a Child of God. It is the portion of the sinner, the ungodly, the wicked, none Christian, those who just go to church that are not born again or repented and Christian who are not living the Christian life, that is, who walk not in newness of life. Even that which he has gathers, God transfers them to the one that is good before Him.

The child of God is to go after the **Wisdom of God, the knowledge of the Holy One and then live a joyful life of praises, adoration and thanksgiving.**

But sadly this is not the life style of many Children of God. Instead they are toiling day and night, turned their jobs and businesses to the god they serve, the devil has successfully deprived many children of God from the easy life God has given to them by making them toil day and night, leaving the principles God has laid down to make their financial lives easier so as to have the chance and time to carry out His work. One of the reasons God is interested in making life easier for us is to enable us carry out his works, as we do His work, more blessings rest upon us, but what do we have today? I don't have chance that is why I could not come for prayer meeting, am on night shift that is why I could not come for Night prayer, I don't have chance that is why I could not go for evangelism, I work on Sundays that is why I can't come to Church, even minister are too busy with their works and businesses to spend quality time with the Lord which makes tremendous power rest upon them to enable them bless the Children of God, they go out very early, work all day and then come home very late and tired, is this the kind of Life Jesus died to bring us into? One of the reasons for our suffering is because we are living the Christian life our ways not God's ways. No wonder many Christians are suffering like the unbelievers. Leaving our responsibilities to carry on us the responsibility of the sinner makes us suffer like them.

The job we do, the business we are involved in and other thing we do to earn money is not what will make us rich as God wants us to be. Whatever it is we do to earn money is an avenue through which God gives us Seeds to sow and bread to eat to sustain us until the time of our harvest - that is; the time of our exaltation. Because of lack of understanding of this, many children of God has turned their job, business and whatever it is they do to earn money as the totality of their lives, some have turned it to their god. Working day and night, leaving home very early and coming back very late without rest even on Sundays and at the end finds themselves spending money on the things they are not supposed to spend their hard earned currency on. Let us apply God's laid down principles to our finances.

"If we live the way they live, we shall see the way they see and what we see is what we get".

This is the invitation for the Child of God;

Isaiah 55 v 1 – 5

55:1 *Ho, every one that thirsteth, come ye to the waters, and he that hath no money; come ye, buy, and eat; yea, come, buy wine and milk without money and without price.*

55:2 *Wherefore do ye spend money for that which is not bread? and your labour for that which satisfieth not? hearken diligently unto me, and eat ye that which is good, and let your soul delight itself in fatness.*

55:3 *Incline your ear, and come unto me: hear, and your soul shall live; and I will make an everlasting covenant with you, even the sure mercies of David.*

55:4 *Behold, I have given him for a witness to the people, a leader and commander to the people.*

55:5 *Behold, thou shalt call a nation that thou knowest not, and nations that knew not thee shall run unto thee because of the LORD thy*

God, and for the Holy One of Israel; for he hath glorified thee.

Do you know that there are some things that many Children of God spend money on that they ought not to? Some they don't need at all and some they need but they are not supposed to buy? Do you know that majority of the things you buy are supposed to be given to you? And if there is any need to buy, you are to buy most of your things lesser than the real prices?

An invitation was proclaimed by God, and the same was re-echoed by the Lord Jesus Christ and you have accepted it and believed it, therefore your life is supposed to be a life of blissful rest.

Matthew 11 v 28 – 30

11:28 *Come unto me, all ye that labour and are heavy laden, and I will give you rest.*

11:29 *TAKE MY YOKE UPON YOU, AND LEARN OF ME; FOR I AM MEEK AND LOWLY IN HEART: AND YE SHALL FIND REST UNTO YOUR SOULS.*

11:30 *For my yoke is easy, and my burden is light.*

Coming to Christ is accepting His invitation which also brings rest to our soul from toiling day and night except you have not taken upon yourself his yoke and neither are you learning of him, if truly you have entered into His rest, then you should cease from your own struggles and applied His wisdom to your life to live a prosperous life.

And again;

Hebrew 4 v 10

4:10 ***For he that is entered into his rest, he also hath ceased from his own works, as God did from his.***

Whatever you do in your life as a job or business for income should be done with rest and struggle free. I say to you, oh Child of God, cease from your struggles now, and let your heart accept the rest that the Lord has given to everyone that believes in Him.

"It is God's desire that we have rest on every side to enable us face the heat of His work, you can't do his work when you are troubled on every side"

God did not give you the ability to travail; your riches are not to be gathered by hard labour, cheating, lying, killing etc. but by ease which comes through the application of the following;

- *WISDOM*
- *KNOWLEDGE*
- *JOY*

The knowledge of Christ and the application of the laid down principles of God is what the child of God must live by. Joy is very important in the life of a Christian. Joy is what we use to fetch water out of the wells of salvation. When a Christian begin to labour hard, spending his / her money on what he / she should not spend it on, frustration comes in which the Preacher termed vexation of spirit. Without Joy, a Christian cannot achieve so many things or receive as it should be. This is one of the reasons God doesn't want us to be sad, anxious or allow our heart to be troubled.

Philippians 4 v 6

4:6 ***Be careful for nothing; but in everything by prayer and supplication with thanksgiving let your requests be made known unto God.***

The word careful there is the same as "**anxious or anxiety**".

John 14 v 1

14:1 ***Let not your heart be troubled: ye believe in God, believe also in me.***

We are responsible for the state of our hearts and minds which controls our moods. We are to guard our hearts so that nothing will affect our hearts negatively. Joy is very essential in our lives; it is joy we use to draw blessing out of the wells of salvation.

Isaiah 12 v 3

12:3 ***Therefore with joy shall ye draw water out of the wells of salvation.***

God knows that if we are labouring day and night, we will be worn out and over stressed which will lead to anxiety, we will not be joyful and as long as the stressful money we are earning is not able to sustain us.

"Anything that steals joy from you directly or indirectly is not of God".

"The cunny attack of a warrior; is to attack his mind".

The joy of the Lord is also our strength - **Nehemiah 8 v 10.** Once joy is diminishing in our lives, the strength of God that works mightily inside us will be reducing, if attention is not paid to it, once it rises to the climax of causing frustration, we will be left with no ability of God inside us. This is also the Genesis of every life of struggles. Before a struggling life begins with a Child of God, the Devil will first of all come for the Joy and anything that brings him / her Joy. This is another reason God does not want us to hang our joy on earthly things that have no foundation. If your affection is on things above, tampering with your joy will be one of the most impossible missions the Devil has ever embarked on. When you are of a joyful heart, praises springs up effortlessly. We need to be joyful to be able to offer effective praises to God which brings God's strength to bears upon our lives.

Psalm 8 v 2

> *8:2 **Out of the mouth of babes and sucklings hast thou ORDAINED STRENGTH because of thine enemies, that thou mightest still the enemy and the avenger.***

Matthew 21 v 16

> ***21:16 And said unto him, Hearest thou what these say? And Jesus saith unto them, Yea; have ye never read, Out of the mouth of babes and sucklings thou hast perfected praise?***

Praising God brings God's strength to you; everything about your life will function by the ability of God. There is no effective praise without a joyful and a grateful heart. Learn to be joyful always and then praise God from the depth of your heart with all your might and strength.

"Exhaust your ability while praising God, your emptiness will be re-filled with the ability of God".

Our Joy is full when we receive what we desire, and then by living a stress free life. The only way we can live the kind of life God wants us to live is to use the **Wisdom, Knowledge** and **Joy** that he has given to us. Seek wisdom, search for knowledge then apply them to yourself with Joy.

Some of these principles you already know, the application is more important. It is good to recognize a problem, the cause, know the solution and how to apply the solution. You may know the problem, which is easy; know what to do which is the solution, applying it is the most important aspect of it. The first of these principles begins in Genesis. Genesis again! I told you a strong argument or matter must begin from Genesis. It's always good when it's from Genesis because it breaks barriers. Nothing in it was given to specific people. Anything from Genesis is for the whole world. Anybody's bubbles can be bursted by it. The death of Jesus

Christ; dying for the whole word started from Genesis. So Genesis is good.

In Genesis, God revealed the secret of multiplication and increase which is termed **"Seed Power"**. So the first financial increase principle is seed power.

SEED POWER

Seed is one powerful, full of potential self-regenerating creature that has self-re-producing life in itself after its kind. The Seed of a plant has life in itself therefore it doesn't need any life from God to grow. All it requires is the right environment. I hope you are not going to ask me, ***"What does seed of a plant has to do with money?"*** If you are asking; then, I'll say everything, seed have money in it. I told you earlier the anointing is all about money now, so I see money in all the scriptures now. Just relax and enjoy this.

Genesis 1 vs 11

> ***1:11 And God said, Let the earth bring forth grass, the herb yielding seed, and the fruit tree yielding fruit after his kind, whose seed is in itself, upon the earth: and it was so.***

In every seed there is a tree and in every tree, there are seeds and in those seeds there are trees. Big thanks to **Myles Munroe** on this subject; I recommend you find the message titled – **Die Empty.**

What we are considering here is that in every seed, there is life and the life in it gives it ability to grow in the rights environment after growing, the tree produces fruits and in those fruits, there are seeds and in those seeds there are trees. The seed power is what beat human philosophy that says; "**A tree cannot make a forest**". It is not true. One seed can make a forest even thousands and thousands and thousands of forests. According to God's structure, one seed is more than a forest. It is also written **"One shall become a thousand" - Isaiah 60 v 22** which is the same principle with **"one shall chase a thousand"- Joshua 23 v 10.** If one seed produces a tree and one tree produces a thousand fruits, multiply the numbers of seeds in those one thousands fruits, then plant the seeds again, you will have one hundred and one trees, what do you think your next harvest would be?. I think you won't only have a forest but forests.

Money is a seed; you say how, did you not understand what we just studied? **"Every seed produces fruit after its kind and in those fruits are seeds also"**. Money grows also to produce more money and the money produced will also produces much thereby moving you from thousand into million and so on.

To make it simpler, when you want to have a harvest of oranges, you plant or sow an orange seed, when it grows, it will produce for you orange fruits, so also when you want to have a harvest of money, you need to sow or plant the seed of money. Still on the principle that says **"every seed after its kind".** When you are asked to sow a seed in church for your financial growth, what do you bring to church to sow? Money, in return you get multiple fold of it. Because God has given every kind of seed life to reproduce after its kind, when you sow money as a seed, you get harvest of money in return. Just the same way you get oranges from an orange tree and inside those oranges there are seeds, in comparism, inside the multiple harvest of money you get by sowing money, there are seeds inside for you to sow more and reap a forest of money (What a revelation?). The certainty of this matter is this; God told Noah that seed time and harvest time shall not seize.

Genesis 8 vs 22

8:22 While the earth remaineth, seedtime and harvest, and cold and heat, and summer and winter, and day and night shall not cease.

So when you sow your seed (Money), your harvest cannot be stopped that's what God is saying. If you want to reap apple fruits you sow apple seeds, if you want to reap orange fruits, you sow orange fruit if you want to reap any kind of fruit, you must sow its seed. So also if you want to reap fruits of money that also have money seeds in them, you must sow money seed so that money tree will grow for you which will give you money fruits which you eat (spend) for your nourishment and also give more seed for you to sow.

"For he gives bread to the eater and seed to the sower".

The problem here is, many don't know how to differentiate their fruits from their seed so they end up eating (spending) both the seed and the fruits, thereby bringing famine (hunger) to themselves.

"Any farmer that eats his seed with his harvest shall have nothing to harvest because he had no seed to sow".

In this book I will differentiate between your seed money and your fruit money. Once you learn it, apply it to your finance.

Your seed can be sown in your life, another person's

life, business or church I did not mention bank, money in the bank profits you very little

TYPES OF FINANCIAL SEEDS

- **Personal seed**
- **An Individual seed**
- **Business seed**
- **Church seed**

I will briefly explain personal seed, individual seed and business seed because our focus is on Church seed.

PERSONAL SEED

Personal seed in the money invested by an individual in himself either through education, craft, acquired skill or any other kind of investment that will profit afterward. The money invested in this is nothing compare with the return in the future. That little money you used is a seed. For example, if someone want to learn tailoring or fashion designing today in Nigeria for a year, the payment and every other things involved till graduation will not amount **₦ 200, 000** at its lowest level, this hand work that you gained with **₦ 200, 000** if well established, has the capacity to yield more than **₦ 500, 000** every year at its lowest capacity, in full capacity it will yield more and the knowledge remains with you forever. The money you used to gain future financial increase is a seed. It is very important to invest in our lives as much as we invest in other things. Educate yourself through schools, acquire skills and discipline in your area of specializations, learn to upgrade yourself. Being a Christian is not a limitation to being the best in your area of specialization. Be the best, be the very best. Invest in yourself, sow seed into your future. If secondary school certificate is what you have, get a job with it and use the money to invest in yourself either to further your education, acquire a skill or start up a business, the factory work money you are earning is not what you should settle your life on, you are to use that little hard earn money to improve yourself, invest in yourself or educate yourself if you truly want to live a financial successful life. I personally recommend all Christians to have one or two businesses, acquired skill or craft, it is easier for God to bless and increase through a personal business of yours than to increase you as a factory worker or working under someone else, working for people is another kind of slavery especially if they are unbelievers, not only is it slavery, it also robes you of your quality time of thinking, planning and time with God, wear you out until you become useless to yourself then they dump you, they are designed to bring your spiritual life down, if your spiritual life is not standing firm, soaring high will be very difficult. That little money you are earning now is a seed to sow for your future; it is not money to buy expensive phone, expensive clothes, expensive home electronics, live expensive life or marry and start given birth on. That hard earn little money that cannot give you the good life you desire is your personal seed, invest it into something that can provide you better income for a better tomorrow.

"If you don't invest in yourself, no one will, it is your responsibility and yours alone".

AN INDIVIDUAL SEED

I am using the term **'an individual seed'** because I don't know the best word to use for now but as I explain you should be able to understand what I am saying. This is an external seed that you sow in another person's life not to the intent that he might repay in the future but just to help the person and look forward for your reward from God. We all don't really get involve into this because we don't understand the importance of it. If you would ask me, I will honestly tell you that investing in others have more reward from God to you than investing in yourself. God doesn't reward you for investing in yourself but owe you when you invest in others, **"I will repay says the Lord".** Why in the world is God interested in us helping others? Because helping other is rendering God's service, announcing to the world that God is good, anyone that receive help from someone they don't know or have connection with praises God for it. Helping others is an act of love, demonstrating the Love of God to humanity which the devil does not like. To frustrate this effort, the devil manipulates the minds of some people you helped against you somehow, someway, sometimes, so as to discourage the act of showing kindness. Many people all around the world have one or two experiences on this, after helping, they were taken for granted, some helped someone whom they thought was stranded on the road which resulted to losing their car and other valuable items, some lost their lives as a result of trying to help others. Anyone that hears such stories finds it difficult to help others again. Actually in the world of today, no one seems to be willing to help someone they don't know because of the evils that have occurred in the name of helping others. As a child of God, you are not to run away from rendering help to people, let who will take you for granted take you for granted, just be wise and listen to the Holy Ghost, he will surely guide your steps in helping others and when he leads you to help, do not hesitate. I love the Lord Jesus Christ; he loves us so much, he told us everything that will happen in this world until the very end, so we are not surprise when we see them happen.

Mathew 24 v 12

> **24:12** ***And because iniquity shall abound, the love of many shall wax cold.***

Don't let your love wax cold because of the evils in the world, don't let the devil win, one of the devil's aim is to completely annihilate or eradicate anything that is a nature of God from the hearts of men, and then he will still be the one accusing us before the father that we are wicked beings. This is war, it is kingdom of light against darkness, let us let our light so shine, that men may see our good works and glorify our father which is in Heaven.

The help we render to others always return to us and our children, be it known unto you that every time you help another person's child, you are sowing a good seed for your own child to reap the harvest in the nearest future. Those whose children hardly find favour are mostly parents who never helped another person's child.

"What you want other to do for you, do it first" .

No matter how rich and wealthy you may be today, somehow some way your child will surely need another person's help which your money, connection and influence may never be able to handle but only the seed you have sown in another child's life will bring the harvest of the solution. Your life and that of your children can never be destitute of favour if you are committed to helping others.

Lending to people can also be difficult because some will borrow and never pay back, the Lord also told us about such who will borrow and never pay back, he calls them "wicked", after which he says " to him that will borrow, **don't turn away if you have it" - Mathew 5 v 42.** Sometimes it is hard to lend people money but if you will listen to the leading of the Holy Ghost, you will be on the safer side, moreover even if they don't pay back, the Lord will pay you back, you have nothing to lose but the one that borrow and not repay has shut the door against himself not from you alone but from anyone connected to the Lord that is in the ministry of lending to people in the name of the Lord Jesus Christ. This is one of the reasons many people don't find a place to borrow money when they need one. The same way financial institutes tag the name of those who borrow money and refuse to pay back through their **BVN, NIN or SSN** which makes it impossible for them to borrow from any other financial institute, so also there is a spiritual tag on those that borrow and not repay.

One day, a woman came to me to borrow some money, as she was explaining to me with the promise of when she will pay back, the Holy Ghost said to me "she will not pay back, nevertheless give her", I smiled, gave her the money, and told the people with me what I heard, till today, she did not pay back and am not offended at it, let the Holy Ghost guide your affairs, you will not fall into a ditch.

"as many as are led by the Spirit, they are the sons / daughters of God".

- **To those that will not pay back, give.**
- **To those that hate you without a cause, give.**
- **To those that seems ungrateful, give.**
- **To those that fights you after helping them, give.**
- **To those that do not deserve it, help and give.**

- **To those who place themselves in the seat of enemy against you, give as long as it is within your power when they come for it especially when the Spirit of the Lord is prompting you to do it.**

✓ **The borrower is subject to the lender.**

✓ **He that lends to the poor lends to me, I will repay says the Lord.**

✓ **Do good to them that hates you.**

If you find yourself in position to help another person's child, don't ignore because the child is not yours, helping another person's child is actually helping your own child just be wise in the affairs of life. Have you ever come across the scripture that says **"the children of the righteous shall not beg for bread?"**

Psalms 37 v 25

> *37:25 I have been young, and now am old; yet have I not seen the righteous forsaken, nor his seed begging bread.*

Do you know why the righteous cannot be forsaken by God nor his children beg for bread? Because the man righteous ***"is ever merciful, and lendeth; and his seed is blessed"*** - verse 26. The righteous is merciful to others and to other people's children, it is not because he is righteous but because he is merciful and lends to others even when they don't deserve it. How does a righteous man shows his merciful acts? By lending to the poor and needy, helping other people's children and showing love to as many as he can reach.

Here is something interesting about the righteous man;

2Corinthians 9 v 9

> ***9:9 (As it is written, He hath dispersed abroad; he hath given to the poor: his righteousness remaineth forever.***

You are a righteous man, learn to disperse abroad to, be the rain of God that falls upon the good and the bad. If you are a married man, explain to your wife and children why it is important, if your wife wouldn't allow you, do it secretly. Always remember every time you have opportunity to sow into another person's life, you are sowing into the future of your lineage.

As much as there is a great reward for anyone that is doing this, there are factors that can affect the blessings from God, if you want God to fully reward your kindness after helping others, you must not do the following;

1. Do not publish your good deeds, don't let everyone know what you did or doing for another person.
2. Don't help others with murmuring and complains, always know that such giving is as though you are giving a seed offering to God.
3. Do not take glory and honour of your good deeds and don't be bitter about someone that did not show you appreciation afterward. If you receive your reward from men, our Lord Jesus says there no reward from God to you; you have taken your reward.
4. Don't hold the people you helped captive or ransom on the account of the help you rendered.
5. Don't wait to be reward in any form by the person you helped.
6. After helping don't remember you helped someone.
7. When you are being appreciated with words, let them know that what you did, you did for the Lord and it is the Lord that works in you both to will and to do of his good pleasures.
8. Be grateful to God for always making provision for you and positioning you to be of help to others when they are in need. See the service as a privilege.

Note: Respect everyone and learn to help elderly people, every single prayer an elderly person prays for you because of a good deed you rendered will not fail in your life. Respect age, anyone older than you should be respected highly and those you are older than should be treated with respect.
If you will discipline yourself in this manner, every single help you rendered will be like a healthy seed sown in a good ground which will produce a harvest of one hundred fold, sixty fold and thirty fold.

May God bless you and increase greatly as you do this.

BUSINESS SEED

Business seed is similar to Church seed but where you are planting your seed is what makes the difference, the same way you need a fertile ground for Church seed so also you need a fertile ground to sow your business seed, the right environment is very important.

Let this sink into you; the seed sowing is investment, both the Church and the Business seed. The money with you is the seed; the business you want to go into is the ground. You must make diligent enquires concerning the business. If it's God that gave the idea, its good but it doesn't mean everything will just go smoothly all the time. Challenges will come, but they that know their God and what He had said; they shall be strong irrespective of the circumstances, these also shall overcome whatever comes their ways. If the business is your own idea, commit it to God and make your enquiries to avoid facing unforeseen problems which may discourage you. But when you know the in and out, whatever comes your way will not be a problem but a challenge which you will overcome.

Note: it is important you take out of your capital that is the money you want to use to start the business and sow in the Church or Minister for the increase, protection favour and ask for wisdom for the business.

WARNING

In these last days, God is not interested in transacting with His children that do not know how to stick with a thing. Many startup businesses and run away from it for one reason or the other. Such a one is like the man Apostle James described as **"unstable",** he says "let not such a one think he shall receive anything from God".

James 1 v 6-8

1:6 ***But let him ask in faith, nothing wavering. For he that wavereth is like a wave of the sea driven with the wind and tossed.***

1:7 ***For let not that man think that he shall receive any thing of the Lord.***

1:8 ***A double minded man is unstable in all his ways.***

Before you go into any business or investment as a Child of God, you must hear from God because once you start it, you are not permitted to run away from it anyhow. So also if it's your decision you are still not permitted to run away from it anyhow. Whatever the challenge may be, face it and deal with it. You have all it takes to win. A word has been given concerning you "**whatsoever he doeth, shall prosper**", except this is not talking about you or you are not walking in the light of it. Moreover, if the owner of that company you are planning to run to for work did not face the heat and overcame, that company will not be standing today.

"Anyone who refuses to take the risk will serve under those who took the risk.

Not only will you serve them, your children will serve them also. When are you going to deliver your family from the bondage of employment? Just like a man working in a factory for a very long time, his own son grows up to be employed in the same factory, the father is a staff; the son is a casual worker. When will someone from your family start employing people?

The purpose of sowing the business seed is to have harvest of multiple incomes. So it's all business, this means to be enriched financially. The children of God are great business men and women. The same way a man can wake up in the morning and take the little money with him to a gambling place and play to win with his faith. So also a child of God with his faith can go to the church, sow his/her money and expect multiple harvests to sow more money. God creates opportunities for His children to make money every day, every hour, every minute, every second, and every month.

"It is God that teaches us to profit"
Isaiah 48 v 17

You may say; is that not going to God to get money? Exactly! That is exactly what it is. Even if I have to steal, I will rather steal from God that has more than enough than to steal from a man. I say if I don't steal from my father, from whose father should I steal? This is not even stealing but taking advantage of the Grace of our Lord Jesus Christ; you see, God loves his children and will do anything to make life easy for them. If any child of God knows how to separate the seed from the fruits for more sowing, he will be very rich without doing much. How simple? You give; you receive more than you gave.

Okay back to business seed - Once you start, the money will begin to produce little money until big money begins to come in. while the small money is coming in, you don't spend them outside the business, keep enduring and keep sowing into the business until the business become a giant business. If you will apply the same principle to church seeding, you will harvest even more than the business harvest.

"If you really want to run business as a Christian, you need to pray for wisdom to run it; it is difficult to survive in business as a Christian without divine wisdom from above"

CHURCH SEED

The church of Jesus Christ has many definitions. I have learned that the meaning of anything is not different from what it is use for. So, for now we will define the Church of Jesus Christ based on what we want to use the church for. We are talking about seed, you and I know fully well that seeds are to be planted therefore I'll defined the Church of Jesus Christ (A place of fellowship) as a ***"fertile ground for sowing seed which has the ability to cause the seed sown to grow healthy trees which produces good fruits resulting in multiple harvests, and more seeds for more sowings"***.

"For a seed to grow and produce a good harvest, the right environment is very important".

When you take your seed to the church, if the church is a fertile church, your seed will grow and will be fruitful, but if the Church is not a fertile Church or ground, the seed may either die or produce degenerated plants which will produce little or no fruits. Now you will want to say does it mean all churches are not fertile ground? I will put it to you this way; do all churches preach Jesus Christ? Is God manifested in all churches? Do all churches believer in the Holy Spirit? You may say yes, then I will ask you if all churches speak in other tongues, I mean the ministry and also filled the members with the Holy Spirit with evidence of speaking in other tongues? Does every church believe in miracles, do all Churches collect tithes? You see all churches are not fertile ground for sowing seed and that does not mean God is not in their midst, it's a thing of belief. A church that doesn't believe in financial prosperity and a church that is against tithing are not a fertile ground for seed sowing, they will eat your money and you will not receive any harvest. More so a Church where the minister does not exercise themselves spiritually to be able to proclaim the blessings of God upon the seed is not a fertile ground, the only difference here is that the seed sowed may take time to grow and produce little or none but the former one will not grow at all.

This seed sowing has some spiritual backups. If you are in congregation that believes when you have money, you won't serve God well, sowing seed there will be a waste of time, money and energy. In every church of Jesus Christ, there is always an anointing based on what they believe and what is being preached there. If your church is against it the anointing to produce will not be there, neither will your money comes to God as a seed, so a fertile ground is important.

How do I know a fertile ground? I just told you. If your church preaches against riches as a worldly thing, giving you backup with the scripture that says **"love not the world nor the things of the world",** it is not a fertile ground for seed sowing. You may say "but it is from the Bible" well the same way the **"Love of money is the root of all evil"** is also in the Bible; "**Jesus was made poor so that we might be rich through his poverty**" is also in the Bible. "**Love not the world"** is not talking about money, it's actually talking about the ways of life of the children of the world; that we should not love their evil life styles nor take pleasure in the evil things they do. Don't love them neither take pleasure in them. The things of the world includes: hatred, envy, wickedness, adultery, fornication, back biting, unforgiveness, evil jesting, murdering, killing, greediness, cheating and any evil way you could think of. These are the things the scripture says we should not love; neither welcome those that do them. The writing that says the "the love of money is the root of all evil" is not in terms of '**be poor and don't be rich'**, It's say; don't be over ambitious because of money, don't make money your priority, don't be greedy of gains, don't live in such a way that you can do anything because of money or to get money, because when you do, you will make yourself eager always to get money at all cost, which may include; stealing, cheating others, killing others, you will become greedy of gains. This is what God doesn't want to see. You will agree with me that as a Child of God you wouldn't want to do anything of such because of money. Your Love is for God and his kingdom, so you cannot allow money to have your Love, the children of the world can do anything to get money, it doesn't matter if a female would need to be naked openly or if a man needs to steal or kill, it doesn't matter to them as long as they will get money in return. No matter how much you are offering a Child of God to be naked publicly, she won't do it neither will the Child of God go to the extreme of killing or stealing because of money. So the scripture is not for a genuine child of God like you because you know better. Is that clear now?

So your seed must be planted in a fertile ground (church). The next thing now is, how do I plant the seed? Take some money out of whatever you have, pray over it concerning what you want it to produce for you and drop it on the altar. Don't give it to anyone. Then keep thanking God for your expectation concerning it.

Let us have a brief calculation of what we should expect;

Mathew 13 v 8

13:8 But other fell into good ground, and brought forth fruit, some an hundredfold, some sixtyfold, some thirtyfold

From here, we can conclude that if a seed is planted on a good ground, it will grow into a tree and a tree is expected to produce;

- **One Hundred fruits**
- **Sixty fruits**
- **Thirty fruits**

Note: Do not limit your faith with these calculations; God is a miracle God, if he considers you worthy, He is able to do exceeding above these calculations. Your relationship with Him is the ultimate.

If your seed is very healthy, out of a good conscience, then expect any of these as harvest but if the ground is not a good ground for seed sowing, you will experience this;

Mathew 13 v 5 - 7

13:5 Some fell upon stony places, where they had not much earth: and forthwith they sprung up, because they had no deepness of earth:

13:6 And when the sun was up, they were scorched; and because they had no root, they withered away.

13:7 And some fell among thorns; and the thorns sprung up, and choked them:

If we sow a good seed in a good ground, God expects us to have whatever we sowed multiplied by hundred, sixty or thirty. But this is not the experience of many Christians, God has given every seed power to grow, God is not the problem but no matter how healthy a seed is, it can produce nothing unless it is planted in the right environment.

The essence of these explanations is to prove to you that the Word of God still works and God is faithful, let us diligently search for a fertile ground for sowing as a good farmer.

"Seed time and harvest time shall not cease"

Note: There is nothing like "Its lack of faith that hindered the desired result". This principle cannot be disannulled after sowing the seed just as a farmer does not need extra faith after planting a seed of corn. Faith is in action and work, the faith part of it is; you believing that when you give it you will receive what you desired according to the principle of seed power which has ability to produce fruits, then fruits with seeds inside. Also God has spoken and it shall not fail; "Seed time and harvest time shall not cease". That means your harvest is sure. The only obstacle you could encounter is the fertile ground which I have explained.

After dropping it, watering is needed, just like every other seed requires rain to grow, so also this kind of seed also need rain to grow. You water your seed with your continuous proclamation, declaration and thanksgiving concerning it. Then give thanks concerning the fruits and the seeds from your harvest.

This principle works!

Note: The Church seed has the ability to produce any harvest for you aside money harvest.

TYPES OF CHURCH SEED

1. Freewill seed
2. Sacrificial seed
3. Compulsory seed

A FREE WILL SEED

A free will seed is a seed that you willingly remove from what you have that you sow to meet a need. This could be a need in the house of God, a need for a Minister, a need for a Brother/Sister in Christ. No one forces you to do this. This kind of seed can be dropped on the altar, offering bags, handed over to the minister or the individual in need of the help. There is always a reward from God for it.

This could be something valuable to you that is needful or something valuable that you no longer need.

SACRIFICIAL SEED

A sacrificial seed is a seed that you sow as a sacrifice for a harvest, increase or multiplication you are expecting, to solve a problem or to avert a problem. This seed is not usually a willing seed. Present needs are also on this kind of seed which makes the person to have very little willingness to sow it. It is a seed sown with expectations. It is not usually sown because you want to, but often sown because you have to. Most of the time, it is sown at a time that is not convenient. This kind of seed is to be dropped on the Altar of the Church or handed directly to the Minister in Church. This must be something valuable and important; your conditions must be clearly stated.

COMPULSORY SEED

A compulsory seed is the seed that is usually levied by the Holy Ghost or Church. This is the seed that is required by the Ministry for the sponsorship of the Ministry's activities, Ministry materials, programs and contributions for some certain reasons. Every member or selected members of the church are usually compelled to give or sow toward one or two things, or committed to some certain financial responsibilities which are not responsibilities they willingly subjected themselves to, many Christians don't give this willingly until a special miracle occurs as a result of the compulsory levy.

The heads of Ministries are more concern about this type of seed than every other seeds because it is majorly used to increase the capacity of the Ministry, offerings and tithes are never enough, every minister is aware that many Christians don't give willingly for other church projects and activities so they rest the Grace of the Ministry upon the arms that they have laid down on which they need the financial contributions of the members. Every other seeds identify you as a Christian but participating in this type of activity (ies) by sowing your seed into them identifies you a member of that Ministry thereby positioning you for the Special blessing and grace that is bestowed on the Ministry. Willingness is good but it is not compulsory, whether it is done willingly or not, the blessing will still be bestowed because it is partnering with the Ministry, in partnership, feelings are not factors but dealing faithfully by giving what you said you would give me if I give this to you (transactions).

A compulsory seed can also be as a result of instruction from the Holy Spirit. You don't have to be happy about it, you just have to do it, and sometimes He won't even tell you why you have to sow the seed. Adhering to this type of instruction will make your life, not adhering to it could destroy your life. Many lives have been saved because they listen and sow this type of seed and many lives have been transformed because they carried out this instruction.

"If you are in a meeting and receive a prompt in your spirit to give a certain amount as seed, don't turn a deaf ear, if you have the money do it".

FACTORS THAT CAN AFFECT THE HARVEST OF YOUR SEED

The following factors determine the harvest of every seed sown;

1. **The health of the seed:-** The health of your seed is measured by your capacity and only God knows your true capacity. If the seed you are sowing is lesser than what God expects of you, your harvest can be affected. But this factor is not a severe factor since what you sow is what you reap, he that sows sparingly shall reap sparingly and he that sows bountifully shall also reap bountifully. So expect your harvest based on the weight of your seed.

   2Corinthians 9 v 6 – 7

   9:6 ***But this I say, He which soweth sparingly shall reap also sparingly; and he which soweth bountifully shall reap also bountifully.***

9:7 Every man according as he purposeth in his heart, so let him give; not grudgingly, or of necessity: for God loveth a cheerful giver.

2. **The Ground:-** The ground here represent the Church, the Minister or the individual you are giving the seed to. If any of these is not a fertile ground, if your seed goes there, the productivity of your seed will be affected which can either reduce your harvest or mare your harvest. This factor is a severe one; the ground on which your seed fall upon can determine how it will produce. Let us learn this lesson from the parable of the sower.

Mathew 13 v 1 –9

13:3 And he spake many things unto them in parables, saying, Behold, a sower went forth to sow;

13:4 And when he sowed, some seeds fell by the way side, and the fowls came and devoured them up:

13:5 Some fell upon stony places, where they had not much earth: and forthwith they sprung up, because they had no deepness of earth:

13:6 *And when the sun was up, they were scorched; and because they had no root, they withered away.*

13:7 *And some fell among thorns; and the thorns sprung up, and choked them:*

13:8 *But other fell into good ground, and brought forth fruit, some an hundredfold, some sixtyfold, some thirtyfold.*

13:9 *Who hath ears to hear, let him hear.*

3. **Watering:-** The watering of a seed sown is majorly the responsibility of the sower but in many cases, the help of the Minister in Charge in watering can speedily increase the growth of the seed and therefore result in bountiful harvest. This factor is 50/50

Here is the summary

- If the seed is good and the Ground is fertile, if there is no adequate watering, the productivity will be affected but still your harvest is sure.

- If the seed is good and the ground is not fertile and there is adequate watering, there will still be harvest but it will not yield the expected harvest.

- If the ground is fertile and there is adequate watering, the seed will produce based on its capacity.

- If the seed is a very healthy one, that is, God sees to it that it's worth more than what you are giving it for or more than you are supposed to sow for the expected harvest, sowed on a fertile ground with adequate watering, there will be bountiful harvest and God shall add increase to the harvest. There shall be net breaking harvest.

HOW TO WATER YOUR SEED

After you have sown a seed, you don't go and sleep, waiting for harvest overnight. No! That is not the way a good farmer does it. A good farmer consistently checks on the seeds he has planted in his farm even though he know it's not yet time for them to grow. Checking to make sure the seeds are not removed from the ground is very important and preventing farm animals is also important to a good farmer.

After sowing your spiritual seed, the next thing you start doing is to do continuous watering. The question here now is; how do I water my seed?
You water your seed by speaking words of your expectations on the seed sown, giving God praises for giving you seed to sow, that He might cause you to reap a bountiful harvest, you pray against anything that can cause your seed not to grow or to hinder the harvest of the seed sown, don't allow negative thoughts about your expectations, the multiplication of your harvest is spiritual and thoughts are powerful when it comes to spiritual activities. Consistently look out for your harvest, understand times and seasons so that you can recognize it when it comes.

Note: Every seed must be sown with a specific purpose which is to be expected at a specific time.

Your heart must be in it, the joy of your harvest must spring up from within you, continuous testimony is important as you earnestly wait for the day of its manifestation.

If you can do this with great excitement, without complaint or murmuring, then you have successfully fulfilled your part as a sower and then a good waterier. If anything happens to your harvest, the ground is to be questioned. But no matter what happen, you cannot lose the whole of your harvest. God is faithful even though the ground has failed you, but the harvest cannot be as it should be. The place of the fertile ground cannot be override. The role of a Minister in the Church cannot be overruled. I don't want to talk about how to make a Church a fertile ground by the Minister in charge here, if a Minister does not know how to make his Church a fertile ground how then can he bless the children of God? Then his Church is not a good ground for sowing, find a good ground for sowing, you can still be worshipping at your church even though it is not a fertile ground.

"Seed time and harvest time shall not cease and we need the blessing of seed time and harvest time".

Any minister that does not know how to make his Church a fertile ground for seed sowing for the Children of God will diminish and those who knows how will increase.

"To him that have more shall be given, to him that have not, even that which he seems to have shall be taken from him".

The Children of God must increase financially; Church is not going to be a barrier to the advancement of the Kingdom. It is part of the blessing.

Note: If your Church is a Church that has good doctrines of salvation, teachings of Paul and the Holy Ghost, you can remain there and be sowing to other ministries, do not cheat yourself by saying my church is my church. No church is your church, let the church that can help you with the help God wants to render to you be your Church. All Churches of Jesus Christ are our Church, don't be like those that say **"I am of Paul and another says I am of Apollos".** Jesus gives ministers gifts for them to perfects and benefits us - **Ephesians 4 v 8**, if the gift you need is not available where you worship and it a serious matter, then you can locate a Minister of Jesus Christ that have it.

Any minister that wants to learn how to make his church a fertile ground for seed sowing should contact me if he is truly serious, I can help.

This is more like the gambling ground of the Children of the Kingdom of God; money doubling avenue.

"The result the children of this world get in the gamble they play is what makes them stick to it even though they know it is not good".

"If you stake well in gamble, your money will double, triple or above, but if you stake wrongly, you will lose your money. Same with your seeding".

"This is our gamble ground; let us learn how to stake well, our winning will be sure".

"The result they get in worldly gambling is one of the reasons they don't want to be converted".

"The result we are not getting from our sowing is what makes them not to believe what we preach to them".

Let us learn how to get the results God wants us to get, then winning the unbelievers will be much easier. They watch us all the time.

I said I will differentiate between your harvest fruits and your harvest seed for more sowing, follow me carefully here; I will try as much as I can to explain this for you to understand.

HOW TO RECOGNIZE YOUR SEED

Sometimes, it is difficult to recognize the seed in our hand, because we don't know sometime, we eat our seed without knowing.

A seed is used to produce harvest, and inside the harvest there are seeds which may not be identified. I said earlier that there are seed inside harvest. Firstly let us look into the seed to be sown for harvest.

RECOGNIZING SEED FOR A HARVEST

A seed for harvest is the seed that you sow for increase. Let us consider the life style of a good farmer then we will be able to clearly understand this. God says; ***"seed time and harvest time shall not cease"***. This means there will always be time to sow. Firstly, we will need to look into '**the time to sow'** and I believe the time to sow can shine light on what is to be sown. Let us use the known to find the unknown.

A time to sow is always a crucial time for every farmer; it is usually a time that there is no much food. Some foolish farmers always eat some of their seed at such a time or all their seeds. Before sowing time, there must be rain, there is always an interval between '**after harvest**' and '**sowing time**'. During harvest, there is usually surplus, but after harvest, food begins to reduce and every farmer will separate some for planting, while waiting for the rain, there is usually little famine. A wise farmer knows that what he has kept for harvest will not sustain him even if he choose to eat it so he endure the hardship until there is rain. But a foolish one won't be able to endure the hardship, instead he will bring out what he had stored for sowing for him and his family to eat and while they are eating they laugh at the wise farmer that refuses to bring out his own that he has reserved for planting. When the time of seed sowing comes, the wise one will have more to sow but the foolish one will have little or none to sow and at the time of harvest, the wise one will have multiple harvests and this is his time to laugh while the foolish one is crying oh God why?

From this, we can understand that before sowing, there is hardship. Hardship on everyone has grade but we all go through hardship one way or the other. I understand that there are great financially buoyant ministers that can say they don't go through hardship but that is not the whole truth either. Some do go through it without recognizing its hardship. Whenever we have a project that what we have is not able to handle it immediately which becomes a burden that must be done within a short period of time, we have to give what we planned to use for something else for it, the time you could not have what you planned to have after diverting the money is a moment of hardship. It doesn't have to last long. Hardship and suffering are two different things. When you spend your salary to facilitates Church projects knowing that there is no food for you and your family, pending the time you are waiting for a miracle, you and your family have to eat or spend the very little that is available; that moment is hardship not suffering and the Bible encourages us to endure hardship as a good soldier **- 2Timothy 2 v 3.**

Back to the subject, there will be hardship before sowing. The hardship time is the time when what you have is not enough to sustain you and your family even if you have to spend it all. Hardship time is when you cannot live luxuriously at a particular time as you used to.

Here is the summary, when what you have is not able to sustain you and your family to be full and remain, it is time to sow.
The law of sowing is to multiply the little you have to produce multiple harvests.

"The money you have that cannot buy what you really need is a seed to sow so as to get a harvest to be able to get that actual thing you wanted".

"What you have at hand that cannot solve a problem that is ahead is a seed to either make the problem not to come or make you prepared for the trouble to come".

"a wise man foresee evil and hide himself from it".

Note: Not all troubles are to be avoided; there are some we need to face for a testimony and for the Glory of the name of Jesus Christ.

"What you have at hand that cannot make you who you want to be is a seed to sow to produce a harvest that will make you who you want to be".

"Whatever level you want to reach, what you have at hand at the level is the seed to produce the harvest that will open the door of where you want to be".

Let us see it this way;
You are working in a company and the salary you are earning is something you cannot seat back and rely on; saying, I have good income, then you are thinking of what you can do to move to the higher level especially when you know you are not qualified to be there due to paper or time limitations. What you do is to give a sacrificial seed, that is; take an amount that cost you something or a whole month salary and say to God, even if I and my family eat this till tomorrow, we will still be hungry, I give this to you, multiply it for me to have a harvest that can sustain me and my family. You know doing this will make the whole house shake that month, endure it with joy. If you have a wife already please carry your wife along, let her understand what you are doing and why you are doing it. When you do this, you are asking God for promotions, if the position you desire is not in that company, the Angels will begin to seek for the opportunity for you elsewhere. This is not supposed to take long but if it does, use the principle of casting your bread upon many waters; sow in the morning, sow at noon and sow in the evening.

Ecclesiastes 11 v 1 – 6

11:1 Cast thy bread upon the waters: for thou

shalt find it after many days.

11:2 *Give a portion to seven, and also to eight; for thou knowest not what evil shall be upon the earth.*

11:3 *If the clouds be full of rain, they empty themselves upon the earth: and if the tree fall toward the south, or toward the north, in the place where the tree falleth, there it shall be.*

11:4 *He that observeth the wind shall not sow; and he that regardeth the clouds shall not reap.*

11:5 *As thou knowest not what is the way of the spirit, nor how the bones do grow in the womb of her that is with child: even so thou knowest not the works of God who maketh all.*

11:6 *In the morning sow thy seed, and in the evening withhold not thine hand: for thou knowest not whether shall prosper, either this or that, or whether they both shall be alike good.*

Give towards other project in the Church or other Churches out of what you are still earning, reminding God why you are doing it. Learn not to grumble or murmur, help your wife also. Make sure you are not complaining in the ear of the Holy Ghost. Stand in the faith that you have demonstrated. You will see your harvest.

Please if you are not ready to follow God whole heartedly until you see a change, don't start it, let this mind be in you which was in Esther ***"if I die I die".*** It is good to be patience with God after you have done what you are supposed to do in matters like this. Where the Angels are arranging for you may be under process or construction. You obtain promises through faith and patience.

Hebrew 6 v 11 – 15

6:11 And we desire that every one of you do show the same diligence to the full assurance of hope unto the end:

6:12 That ye be not slothful, but followers of them who through faith and patience inherit the promises.

6:13 For when God made promise to Abraham, because he could swear by no greater, he

sware by himself,

6:14 *Saying, Surely blessing I will bless thee, and multiplying I will multiply thee.*

6:15 *And so, after he had patiently endured, he obtained the promise.*

Aside sowing seed for multiple harvest, increase, promotion and supernatural desires, there is also need to sow seed to avoid troubles especially when you know if things go sideways, you are finished. It's not everything that comes your way your personal faith can carry especially if the life of another person is involved. If it's you alone that is involve; it's okay to rely on your faith because you know the measure of your faith and what you can do with it.

For instance, when my wife was pregnant, I knew it's more than just being pregnant and delivering. Before the pregnancy, the parents and the family members had been a great objection to our relationship, they went extra mile of disgracing my family members when we came to them but yet could not stop us. Now that she is pregnant, I knew they are wicked enough to see that as an opportunity to deal with this man they just could not defeat for many years. I called my wife; I asked her, what do you want? Should we prepare some money for operation or you will deliver through normal process? She said; "I will deliver through normal process". With this I had her consent which is very important in the spirit real. Then I proceeded to my side, I have faith for sure, but just having faith is not enough on some sensitive matters. I spent time with God and recounted one by one what will be affected in His Kingdom if anything goes amiss. I made God understand if anything happen to her, He still remain my God but the works He has committed into my hands will be delayed if not abandon (**"It is good to be relevant to God"**). And the Lord said to me; **"I will do you good".**

My responsibilities to Him was not enough, I went on to make a vow of what I will give as a seed for her safe delivery, then I pressed on with prayers, positioning myself for the victory, to deal with fear and every other limitation that could make me limit God in His work on her safe delivery. I fasted and prayed as I had my spiritual eyes open watching to see whatever will intend to interfere. This was more than just birth; the whole of the Ministry the Lord commissioned into my hands was at a big threat including all the books that we are publishing now. I just couldn't afford to take any defeat. It was a Kingdom against a Kingdom!

Then came the day of labour, it was on Sunday night, I was with her, she complained bitterly of some strange pains I laid my hands on the baby and asked if she was ready to come out, she kicked me, I took that as a yes, then I asked if she could give me two more days to quickly round up the necessary arrangements I was making for her coming, she kicked my hands again, then I said fine. I told my wife it's late already, by tomorrow morning she should be going to the Hospital. I returned to my house (we were not living together; I sent her to her parents' house when her delivering time was getting closer since I don't know much about what to do in time of labour). Later in the night, her sister called me that my wife is complaining of pains bitterly and this was around 11pm, I went there and told her to go to the Hospital with her sister. I went back home to continue my cleaning. After a while, I went to the Hospital, carried her things and made necessary payments after which, I came back home to finish the arrangement, gave thanks to God, and then went to sleep. Should in case you are wondering if I was sleeping while my wife was in labour, yes! That is what I did, I went to sleep. Sleeping at such a time as this was the best thing I could do to allow God perfect His work, I have done all that is necessary, it's now God's turn, so I slept very well, woke very early in the morning to go to the Hospital, she was already in delivery room. The Matron was not happy that I was not there with her all night, well if I was there with her, her cry of pain may bring me to the valley of pity which will affect my faith and God needed my cooperation in faith and the best way to do that is to be absence, so I was not being wicked but was applying spiritual principles. As at the time I got there, she has lost strength to push and the matron was already considering referring her to another Hospital for operation that I did not prepare for. My pastor was in consistent communication with me, I started praising God, it wasn't long, strength came to her after a while I receive a prompt in my spirit that this is the time, then I began to talk in other tongues, five minutes after, a cry of a baby was heard, I shouted Glory to God, fell to the ground and worshiped Him. If there was no miraculous intervention, my wife could have given up on pushing! No more strength to breath.

You see why I said, having faith and say I believe is not enough especially if the life of another is at stake? You have to demonstrate your faith by acting in lines with principles that will make you stand on the Ground that God is in control. You don't just say God is in control and I have faith when there is no strong hold binding you and God together. I had the following as proof that God is in control;

- **His word - I will do you good**
- **His works in my hand**
- **My faith in Him**
- **My vow and my Seed**
- **My prayers and Fasting with thanks giving**
- **Holding my peace to let Him do what I cannot do.**

With this simple analysis, you can understand why many don't get what they are expecting from God if all they are using is faith. When you need serious turn around, I have faith is never enough, demonstrate your faith by making a vow or sowing a seed for your expectations.

Let me also share this testimony with you, may be it will help you understand what I am saying.

When my sister died, we took her body to our home town, my elder brother was very angry because the husband did not know any of us including me that live very close to them, my brother and the rest of the family insisted that he must carry out wedding ceremony with my dead sister which thing I was against, I fought them all until wedding a dead body issue was cancelled, I was able to convince the man and his family that nothing will happened to them, when we got to the village, I called my elder brother that we have arrived, while talking to me on the phone, he called my little brother to bring his dagger (knife) for him thinking I have hung up, he did not know that I heard him, I hanged up immediately, call the man and my brother with me and started running, they just followed me not knowing why I was running, when we got to a good place, I told them my brother was going to kill the husband of my late sister and I don't want any blood to be upon us. I was so afraid, not because of myself but because of the man, I persuaded him to come and if anything happen to him, it will seem as if I deceived him so as to have him killed. The whole family gathered, they began to call me to come back with the man, I told them I can't as long as my elder brother is aiming at killing him, I had to go first, while I was going my heart was greatly troubled, I knew within me a terrible thing will happen, I lifted my voice to God and prayed a very short prayer, I said; "oh God, my heart is greatly trouble, my bones are out of joint, my heart is failing me because fear, deliver me and everyone that comes with me to this village, if you will help us and bring us back to our destination safely, I will give so so and so as a thanks giving offering". After praying, I went to meet the family, they promised to make sure nothing happen to him, I then sent for the man, when he arrived, then came the mighty hand of God. How He miraculously touched my brother's heart to the extent that the same person that wanted to kill this man later became the person that helped him lightened the burden of expenses the whole family laid on him, my brother became the very Angel God used to help us finished all the necessary ceremony that same night, made arrangement for her grave and organized the people that buried her as though this was not enough, he also gave us money the next day to spend on our way back to Lagos, he said; "I know you don't have much money on you anymore".

May be if I have depended on my faith that day, the worst would have happened, faith and fear don't work together, you can't be terribly afraid and still stand in faith, I was heavily dis-jointed because it was about another person's life. Sometime, I have faith is not enough, a seed offering or sacrificial offering is needful. The Bible says; ***"Hast thou faith? have it to thyself before God". - Romans 14 v 22,*** don't jeopardize another person's life in the name of demonstrating your faith.

HARVEST FRUITS AND YOUR HARVEST SEEDS

When you sow your seed either in business or in Church, you will definitely receive harvest, the harvest is fruit, just like plants, and in these fruits are seeds which you should not eat. The harvest money you receive as a result of the seed you sown, is your fruit, now that fruit have seeds inside, that is, the money you receive, you are not to spend all of it for yourself; you should remove out of it, this time more than you sow before and sow again. You are to sow more than before because your harvest is already more than the seed you sown before.

For Example, you plant one seed of orange, the seed grows into a tree, and the tree bear orange fruits. If you are familiar with crops you will realize that fruit trees don't produce much fruit at first. Now what we are saying is; you pluck those few oranges which are your first harvest, drink the water inside, remove the seeds and plant all the seeds. You will surely have more seeds. Let's assume the numbers of oranges are five, inside each orange you find three seeds, three multiply by five will give you fifteen, so your one seed of orange has given you fifteen seeds which you can sow again to get fifteen trees of oranges plus the other one; you have sixteen trees of oranges. By the time these sixteen trees of oranges produces again; you will have a basket full at least. Now multiply three seeds by the numbers of the oranges in the basket, wow that has just made you an orange producing company. This is the same thing with Church seed, even business seed. When you receive harvest from church seed, the first seed is not dead; you will still be receiving from it till Jesus comes. That is why sometimes we may not give much in church financially after much giving for a long time but miracle money and financial opportunities keep coming. You can do more, how much you want to receive depends on you.

If you have been following me whole heartedly, you will observe that I have not talked about prayers. This one is not prayers. This one is not prayer work;

if it's prayer work; then prayer warriors would be the richest in the kingdom. But it's surprising to know that some of the people who stumble into these principle and give in churches or for anything that pertain to the Ministry of Jesus Christ do receive financially. Some of them don't even have time to study the Bible or pray. This has nothing to do with prayers. When it's time of prayer I will tell you.

So keep sowing and keep harvesting. Don't forget any Church that has problem with Christian being rich is not a fertile to sow. Well there is another way of knowing them. They are religious Churches professing to be the most holy Christians, they justify themselves by their works and lay rules for the members which are not Jesus' rules. Such Churches don't grow; you will never hear testimonies of financial or spiritual success. The second kind of this is the Church of Ministers that are not exercising their selves spiritually; some are just there for the money while some are just lazy. If you sow seeds in a Church and you do all that is in your part and it does not produce what it should produce at the time it should, then start having a second thought of another church for seed sowing, God is aware of this problem that is why we are instructed by the Spirit to cast our bread upon the waters not water.

Ecclesiastes 11 v 1 – 2

11:1 Cast thy bread upon the waters: for thou shalt find it after many days.

11:2 Give a portion to seven, and also to eight; for thou knowest not what evil shall be upon the earth.

This is not moving from one Church to another, this is searching for a good ground to sow. You may remain in your Church and be giving for financial needs in other Churches or Ministries of Jesus Christ. Let this sink inside you; your Church is not the only Church of Jesus Christ on earth. Every Church of Jesus Christ has financial responsibilities to play on earth before rapture and if we are truly the seed of Abraham, then it should show. Many Churches don't care whether you received the blessing attached to seed sown or not. It is the responsibility of the minister to see to it that your request is granted. They are not there to collect the money alone; they are to make sure the blessing follows. Don't settle for less. Strive; there is more than enough for you and me. Let's go about it God's ways. So far I don't think I have mention anytime outside what is written in the word of God.

RECOGNIZING SEED IN YOUR HARVEST

After receiving harvest of the seed you have sown, there is need to sow again. The question now is, how can I recognize my seed inside this harvest since the seeds in a harvest are not to be eaten? Firstly you need to recognize your harvest. Recognizing a particular answer to a particular prayer makes us have confidence in prayer and in God. Many Christians pray and don't recognize it when the answer to their prayers comes; I am not dealing with prayer now, so I don't want to go there. Here is what I am saying; many Christians sow seeds and forget they sow a particular seed for a particular purpose, when the harvest comes, they won't be able to recognize it by and by they eat the harvest and the seeds. This is not good enough, blessed is the man whose heart is in his giving; know what you are doing and cautiously do it with the understanding. When you sow a seed, expect a harvest, when the harvest comes, it will be able to fix the need that made you sow the seed and then will leave you with excesses, from the excesses, you have more seed to sow again. The seed in your harvest is the excess or in the excess, depending on how you want it. All of the excess or some of the excess for your next sowing.

For example: your rents will be due soon and you know with the way salary or income is going, you may not be able to get the money on time to pay, so to avoid embarrassment, you decide to give a seed for the harvest of money that will pay the rents for you. Let us assume the rent is ₦100,000 per year. The harvest is to come at the time the rent is due or few days, weeks or month after. When the money comes, it will surpass the rent payment, after paying the rents, you will have extra with you. You should take out of the extra for thanks giving and to sow again, for the something else, it is good to sow from that harvest again; this is also applicable to Business seeds.

Note: All seeds must be tithe free. You must remove your tithe from any money you want to use to sow as a seed. Tithing helps to sanctify our money.

Note: Sometimes harvest may come through ideas and opportunities that will make you receive the harvest of the seed you sow.

Just as there are different types of plants, so also there are different kinds of seed. All plants do not produce within a short time; some take months, and some years before production. Learn to name your seed and the time of its production to avoid the Angels deciding that for you without your notice which may fall at the time you may not like even though it's still for your good. If your seed is planted on a fertile ground, there is nothing stopping it from growing and then your harvest is sure. I am aware of some that have sown seeds and it did not produce harvest at the time it should, do not be discouraged, even if it takes time, you will surely reap your harvest. Hold on to this word; **"what a man sow, he shall reap".** Let's move on to the second principle which is tithe.

TITHE

Tithe is the second principle to be revealed after seed power. Tithe was revealed in the days of papa AB (Abraham) when he met a being that existed without being born, no father, no mother, no birth date, no death date. What a man! His name forevermore is Melchizedek. Can you imagine? A man living without brother, sister, father even mother, how then did he get here on earth? The marvelous works of God! remind me so that I can ask our Lord Jesus when we get to Heaven about this great man, I have so many of such questions to ask Him that I have not found answers to here on earth.

So let's get going. Papa AB went to rescue his cousin who was captured by the kings that invaded the land where Lot lived. Papa AB and his household fought against five Kings and defeated them. He brought back Lot and his family. On his way back he met this priest Melchizedek whom he paid tithe to. This is where tithe was first revealed.

Genesis 14 vs 18-20

14:18 And Melchizedek king of Salem brought forth bread and wine: and he was the priest of the most high God.

14:19 And he blessed him, and said, Blessed be

Abram of the most high God, possessor of heaven and earth:

14:20 *And blessed be the most high God, which hath delivered thine enemies into thy hand. And he gave him tithes of all.*

Abraham gave this man tithe. So you see tithe was revealed also in Genesis. For detailed study on Melchizedek, study the following scriptures;

Genesis 14 vs 14 – 20

Hebrew 7 vs 1, 5 vs 6

Psalm 110 vs 4

Micah 6 vs 6

Act 16 vs 17

The calculation of how Abraham gave his tithe to Priest Melchizedek was not made known here until Jacob faced the greatest fear of his life.

Genesis 28 v 20 -22

28:20 *And Jacob vowed a vow, saying, If God will be with me, and will keep me in this way that I go, and will give me bread to eat, and raiment to put on,*

28:21 *So that I come again to my father's house in peace; then shall the LORD be my God:*

28:22 *And this stone, which I have set for a*

pillar, shall be God's house: and of all that thou shalt give me I WILL SURELY GIVE THE TENTH UNTO THEE.

Tithe and how to calculate it was revealed here. This is where the theory of 10% came in but the importance was not revealed until the days when the children of Israel refused to pay their tithe. Thank God for prophet Malachi, if not for him we will not have a definite importance of tithe, the argument will not have a definite answer. Through this prophet God told the children of Israel about John the Baptist who will prepare the way for the Lord Jesus Christ. And you and I know the words came to pass. All that is written in **Malachi 3 vs 1**, Jesus whom you and I believed in today testify to this in **Mathew 11 vs 10, Mark 1 vs 2, Luke 1 vs 76**, go through all these scriptures. Do you know the reason for taking you through this? Who is saying something is important. What we hear matters and who is saying it matters more.

This Malachi spoke those words concerning John the Baptist even the coming of the Lord, and Jesus attested to those words in the New Testament. So Malachi is worth listening to and obeying his instructions because he is God's oracle indeed.

Malachi 3 vs 6-12 but I will pick out 10, 11 and 12.

3:10 *Bring ye all the tithes into the storehouse, that there may be meat in mine house, and prove me now herewith, saith the LORD of hosts, if I will not open you the windows of heaven, and pour you out a blessing, that there shall not be room enough to receive it.*

3:11 *And I will rebuke the devourer for your sakes, and he shall not destroy the fruits of your ground; neither shall your vine cast her fruit before the time in the field, saith the LORD of hosts.*

3:12 *And all nations shall call you blessed: for ye shall be a delightsome land, saith the LORD of hosts.*

Hold on for a moment, this prophet was not a priest, if he was one of the priests, we could say, he is saying this to make the children of Israel bring tithe for him to eat. He does not have a share in tithe at all. So paying attention to this is important, just as I am talking to you about this now, I am not your Pastor neither am I a Pastor yet to eat your tithe. I don't think you can beat me in this matter, I pay my tithe. I am not saying the amount; I am saying the way and manner.

God says bring all the tithes, after bringing it, He said, wait and see if I will not pour out a blessing on you. Hey! A blessing, I thought all the seeds of Abraham are blessed? Here you realize tithe has its own blessing and not the general blessing. After blessing, God said something else; I will rebuke the devourer. What does it mean? Because of your tithe I will rebuke the devourer? Does this mean there is a devourer (waster, destroyer) in finance if a tithe is not paid? Yes. That is what God says, so who is this devourer? The devourer is a spirit (Evil) that creates scene that causes people to waste money. You want to know how? I'll tell you something you will go out and find out too.

The major cry of the natural man out there is, **"I am making money and I don't know what I am doing with it** "or once money enters my hand something useless will come up and finish the money, hmm! These are some acts of the devourer. Some says; **"once I have money that is when my wife or child gets sick"** after spending the money, the child gets well. Devourer! Some may mistakenly cause damage to somebody's property that will not let them go except they pay. Devourer! Some are enticed with shallow things like drinking. (You may not drink much but will surely buy for others). There is a spirit of oneness in smoking and drinking. No selfishness in it, you have to buy for others, whether you like it or not. This will make you spend money than you actually wanted to spend, Devourer. Looking for financial favour everywhere, everywhere you go no help; Devourer! Not only, does it waste, what you already have, it also takes away beauty of favour from you and drain you of any idea that will cause you to make money. Everywhere you go, no one will want to help you.

One day I was talking with someone along this line, he said once money enters my hand, I don't know how it always disappear, I end up spending it anyhow on unprofitable things, I may probably give it to people who don't even spend it on something good. I told him well, that is not my experience, any money that enters my hand has come to stay and if I spend, I spend it on what I planned on it and send it on a message and it will come back to me when next I need it because God has made my hands a home for money to stay. I was not making this up, it's actually my lifestyle and it's still in my lifestyle. If you are experiencing wasting of money or money is not coming to you as suppose, then you have to do check and balance. Almost every child of God hears about tithe every day, because you cannot separate

Pastors from tithe (it's their rights). The problem about tithe is not really the payment but how we pay it, that is what matters. I will explain to you very soon how God's Spirit taught how to pay tithe. Prior to this time, I taught I was doing it well, after He (Holy Spirit) taught me, I realized how much of God's money I had eaten. I said Lord forgive me for robbing you. I was surprised at what I took to church and what I still take to church as tithe afterwards.

HOW TO GIVE / PAY TITHE

Let's hear my story, when I was working as salary earner, at the end of the month, I will take one tenth of my salary; that is ten percent of it. For example if my monthly salary is ten thousand my tithe is one thousand this is how it should be removed. This is how many of God's children pay their tithes. This method is for those who just want normal life. That is living from hands to mouth. I know this may sound irritating to your hearing but anyone paying tithe in that manner cannot grow. You are like a man who is saying to God "**give me neither riches nor poverty**", when you pay tithe in this manner, you will not lack yet you will not have more than enough. Whatever you are earning will hardly sustain you and your family. Like I said earlier, don't get upset with me before you finish this book, I will surely reveal hard matters that may not sound nice to you. I used to pay tithe the same way, that is; wait for month to end then remove one—tenth of whatever I have and pay as tithe, so I am just putting this on you. Let's see why that method of paying tithe is not profitable for growth before I tell you my story of how the Holy Spirit taught me how to pay tithe.

When you are waiting to remove your tithe at the end of the month and remove the one-tenth of it, I said, you will never grow up financially that way, because you are limiting yourself and at the same time, robbing God somehow. Now you say how am I limiting myself? Is that not what the scripture says? Well the scripture did not say one-tenth of your salary, but one-tenth of all your increase! Aaah let's see the scripture again.

Malachi 3 vs 10

3:10 ***Bring ye all the tithes into the storehouse, that there may be meat in mine house, and prove me now herewith, saith the LORD of hosts, if I will not open you the windows of heaven, and pour you out a blessing, that***

there shall not be room enough to receive it.

You may say where the "All your increase? I told you earlier that, there is a difference between a man that read the Bible and a man that study the word of God **(I study to show myself approved unto God)**. If you have a center reference Bible **(King James)** it will help if not try to get one. If you have a center reference King James follow me to **Malachi 3vs10.**

Before **"Bring ye all the tithes"** there is a small **(r),** the (**r**) is immediately after 10, before the B of Bring; Have you seen it? If you have, good, let's move on. There are two lines in the middle of the Bible (Centre Reference King James), locate 3vs10, once you find it, the first reference in that **Malachi 3 vs 10**. Will be denoted by that small (r) at the front, you will see **Proverb 3 vs 9**, after that, you will see (s) having **1Chronicles 26 vs 20**. Go back to the main content in that **Malachi 3 vs 10**; you will see the small (s) at the back of **"the storehouse"**. The (r) which is before "Brings" means that (r) is what will be used to trace any scripture that is talking about "Bring ye all the tithes into" after the "**into**" is small (s) so the content of the small (r) is from "**Bring" to "into**" that is the scripture, that is; that (r) will be used to reference it because the content "Bring into" is centered on tithe, so tithe is the subject. Now in-between the two lines again, locate 3:10, the first reference there begins with (r) because in that chapter 3:10 you will see the small (r) at the front you will see proverb 3:9, in other words, proverb 3:9 is in line with Malachi 3:10 ("Bring ye all the tithe into"

Let's see proverb 3:9
Honour the lord with thy substances and with the first fruits of ALL THINE INCREASE.

We could say we want to take out honour the lord with thy substances" alone if the small (n) which is at the back of 'so' is after since that is behind "and with the first fruits". But the small (n) is before **"so"**, which is verse 10. In other words from "Honour—increase is talking about the same thing. I am not dealing with first fruits here so I would not want to emphasize on that, we will talk about it later. What I want to bring out here is "of all thine increase". Since Malachi 3:10 referenced to this, it means your tithe is the one—tenth of all thine increase. The strong argument here is **"all thine increase".** What does it mean **"all thine increase"**? it means anything that enters into your hand as an addition every day, every minute, every second, that was not in your possession before, once it enters your possession, the scripture says; it's an increase, so on every increase, there is a tithe in it that must be removed.

For example:- you wake up in the morning you have some money with you to get something, if peradventure, someone comes in, and give you another money, the money given to you is an increase, so tithe ought to be removed from it before you spend it. Or maybe someone buy you something, that is an increase you should find out the amount that can buy whatever it is that is given to you then pay the tithe. From here, I believe, your heart is doing calculations already on things you get before your salary comes in. When you remove the exact amount of tithe from your salary, whatever it is that you had received before your salary was paid, you did not pay tithe for it by doing this, you owe God, cheating yourself and discouraging Angels from making people give you things.

This is similar to what Papa Job was doing. Job would offer sacrifices to God on behalf of his family, while offering his supplications to God, he would say; **"perhaps my children have commit a sin that I don't know of"**, so he would offer sacrifices ahead. What am I saying? You are supposed to pay more than the regular amount of your tithe. When you pay more than what you are supposed to pay as tithe from your salary, you are either paying for what you've already eaten and did not know or you are paying for higher amount more than your previous salary that is equal the amount for the tithe you paid. So whether you are determining to grow financially or not, it's good to pay more than you think you should, peradventure, you may be clearing your outstanding debts.

Let's talk about the higher level of tithes. Like I said, the monthly method is what I was using also, before we proceed, let's look carefully into this matter.

What is tithe use for? Tithe is use for the things of God, if tithe is use for the things of God that means, the rent of the church, the minister ware fare, the whole financial activities of the Church rests on the tithe, now consider your own Church and calculate how much tithe you pay in a year and see what it can accomplish, then see what you have done for yourself over the year. You will realize that you have given very little for the work of God and this is not profitable for any Child of God.

"Where the treasure of a man is, there will his heart be also".

"Those who give big get big reward".

One day, I was listening to a minister teaching along the line, as he was teaching, I said, Lord, I want to know more about this tithing thing. Right there the Holy Spirit opened my understanding and explains to me how to pay tithe, I am glad to show you these glad tidings.

He made me to understand that any money given me, even though is a free gift, tithe should be removed when I collect money for job done or business transaction, the profit that is mine should not be spent without removing tithe from it. After saying this, I said to him, how come you did not let me know this all this while? He said; "you did not ask me questions about it". Before this time, I do have envelope where I put my tithe monthly before taking it to Church. I told myself I am going to make adjustment to this. The next day being Monday, I took a book and record all the sales and the incomes. I removed the tithe of it and put it in my tithe envelop. The next day I did the same thing. At the end of the month, I realize a big difference between what I used to take to Church as tithe monthly and what I have as a result of daily removal of tithe.

Whatever enters my hand, I remove tithe from it immediately before spending it. Sometimes I remove it from money that does go out for expenses. I don't

just remove tithe from money at hand as profit, I remove tithe from money that comes in, whether is going for expenses or am using it for something else. When you remove tithe in this manner, you are saying to God ***"all this money is what I want to be earning as profit"***. This is a means of paying tithe that promotes you and whatever you do financially.
Let me show you a little secret. Did you know you could accumulate so many properties by paying the tithe of the worth? Listen to the Spirit carefully, you can get something at its tithe rate; do you get it? What I am saying is that what someone else paid **N100, 000** to get; you can get the same with just **N10, 000** naira. This can happen in two ways; either someone give you something worth **₦ 100, 000**, then you take a tithe of **₦ 10, 000** to God with thanks giving offering or you could pay a tithe of **₦ 10, 000** and expect whatever it is you desire that is worth **₦ 100, 000**. This is exactly what God wants for us, am sure if this work for us all, every one of us will enjoy the blessing of tithe as it should be. The possibility of this depends so much on the Ministry and the Minister you paid the tithe to.
Note: Any money you want to use to pay for tithe of an expected harvest must be tithe free. Make sure you remove tithe from it.

Most Children of God are tired of paying tithe especially those that knows the blessing that should follow, whose heart are in their tithing because it seems is only the Minister that is enjoying it, the purpose of introducing tithe by God is to enrich his Children and not the Minister, it is majorly for the benefit of the Children of God because the Minister is to receive one part and the child of God takes the remaining nine, the Minister seems to be enriched by it because of the number of the people paying it to him but if we individually receive the blessings of tithe and pay tithe at advanced level, we will gain tithe more than the Minister that collect tithe. Let us learn how to pay it so that if anything goes wrong in the blessing, we will know where to look into.

BREAKDOWN FOR SALARY EARNERS AND BUSINESS OWNERS

Let me give you a breakdown of this; if you are a salary earner, removing tithe will be very easy. You have three ways of removing your tithe;

1. Removing tithe from anything you received that you should or could have purchase with your money and then at the end of the month you

remove the exact amount of tithe from your salary.

2. You can pay your tithe at the end of the month based on your salary and additional to represent every other money, gifts or items you could have paid for that was given to you.

3. Remove tithe from whatever you receive as present, and then pay more than your usual tithing amount for promotion of a position where the amount of which you paid tithe for is paid.

Note: When you learn to remove tithe from items received that are valuable, you will be opening doors for more to come to you.

If you are a business man that receives money daily, you can be removing your tithe daily, all you need to do is to have an envelope just like me, write tithe at the back of it and keep it somewhere safe. After the daily record, you can decide how you want to pay your tithe and pay it weekly, either ways is fine with God. Don't deposit it in your account, it becomes very difficult to remove sometimes because something may come up for you to spend money on, because of the urgency of the matter, you may end up withdrawing your tithe alongside with hope of removing it later which you may not remember the former.

Note: don't let your tithes accumulate too much; it will be difficult to remove it since business always wants money to be put in it, pay it weekly or monthly if you can separate it and keep it.

1. You can choose to pay your tithe after calculating all your income and then deduct all necessary expenses. So your tithe will be based on your profit. This is also fine with God, but it has limitations for you. The amount you will have as cash at hand will definitely be lesser than the total income. This means your tithe won't amount much, and this is not good for a business you are expecting to grow miraculously.

2. You can choose to remove tithe before expenses. For example; if your business is a business that people patronizes every day, you may need fuel for generator, staff payment or feeding allowances. Whatever the expenses is, you will surely calculate the amount of money that came in first before removing total expenses in a situation where the staff will be paid at the end of

the month, and your record could be daily, weekly or monthly. After calculating the total money that came in for the day, week or month you can remove your tithe from all the money that came in, this helps to move your business to higher level. This is fine with God.

3. You can also choose to pay tithe of all the money that came in throughout the day, week or month and add extra. This helps your business to grow higher and higher, with more security Angels, favour, and doors of ideas to increase the business. This is also fine with God. When you relate with God in your tithes like this, anyone that rises against you through your business is in trouble.

   Note: if you choose to remove your tithe before deducting staff's monthly salary and other expenses is better, you will not only be increased for doing that, your staff will be blessed also even though they still have to remove their own tithe if they are Christians. After removing your tithe, the remaining money is all yours.

Now why is it better to remove tithe before removing expenses and salaries? It is better because, the amount you will be paying as tithe will be huge compare to what it would have been if expenses and salaries are removed. Now that your tithe is huge, your turnover according to the blessing of tithe is multiply by ten.

The equation is simple:-

High tithe = High turnover

Low tithe = Low turnover

Your tithe X = 10

Your amount X multiply by 10 = your harvest

Total income = 100, 000, expenses 30, 000

Cash at hand = 70, 000, tithe will be 7, 000

Your next harvest, your will have 70, 000, as income after expenses. Irrespective of how much you made, expenses will beat it down to what you paid for, somehow you may make more, as your income increases, your expenses will increase also, and somehow, something will always happen to keep you at that level.

But if your total income = 100, 000 and expenses is 30, 000 and you decide to pay 10, 000 as tithe, your total income may increase or remain the same but something will happen that will cut your expenses

down to make sure you have the whole of 100, 000 to yourself.

The amount of your tithe will always be multiplied by **10** since you are using **10%** to pay. When you grow from **10%,** calculation for you will also change. Some people that work in companies that maintain 10% based on their income hardly enjoy the blessing because they will only be secured in the job and be free from unnecessary expenses but the increase will not be there.

Don't forget tithe is not a religious thing; it is a partnership between God and his children in whatever they do to earn money. When you give tithe, you receive a blessing that goes with tithe.

What a man sow, that he shall reap.

We studied two scriptures about tithe; both of them talk about the blessing that follows.

Malachi 3 vs 10 and **Proverbs 3 vs 9**, these two scriptures talk about tithe and the reward that follows.

Did you know that in real spiritual sense we ought not to be waiting for God to reward us when we pay tithe? You pay tithe of what He (God) has already blessed you with. Some people have miss-used tithe. They try to hold God to do something for them because they pay tithe. This is wrong; I don't blame the Christian that try to tell God; ***"you have to bless me or give me something because I pay my tithe"***. The ministers made it obvious. When a member comes to a Minister needing help, they start by checking tithe records, they make tithing issue as the only license to get God. Well it is true that some things are not supposed to, but I am happy for you if you pay your tithe regularly; but what I am saying here is, if there is any reason we should ever use to hold God and demand His interference, it should not be anything lesser than the finished work of Jesus Christ. If there is any reason God cannot say no to us in our request, it should be because of what Jesus Christ did on the cross not small things like tithe which you could not even pay as you should. I say we are not supposed to hope for special blessings based on our tithe because tithe is God's share in partnering with you. What I mean is this. Tithe is one-tenth of all your increase right? You must have the money before you can remove your tithe. God made provision for you, He says, take nine parts and give me one part. Who is doing who favour? If there is any need to boast who should boast? God should, because He gives you more and he take less. In another sense, tithe is like you and someone who do business together, at the end of the day, the profit made is divided among the two of you, and you take nine thousand and the other person take one thousand who owes who? You owe him because He gives you more. It will be foolish if you are expecting him to thank you. If there is anybody who should say thank you, you should be the one. We should be grateful to Him for giving us nine parts and taking one part. Because tithe is God's share for partnering with you, it's one of the major reasons He says; **"you robbed me"** when you don't give Him.

Let me show you one of the things that happen when you don't pay your tithe. Two men came out agreement to work together and have an establishment, one of them is to sit in the office, the other is to go out there and do marketing, tell people about the business and to direct and bring customers to patronize the business, at the end of the day they made good money. Then when the time to share money came, the one out could not come to the office, he was still out there dealing with people, persuading them to come and buy products from the establishment, so he sent a messenger (Minister) to collect his share from the one in the office, the one at the office then refused to send the money of the one doing marketing. Later he returned to the office. He asked his partner, where is my share? The partner who always sits at the office gave excuses why he could not spare out his share, the marketer got angry and felt disappointed; he regretted his contribution to the business. Finally, he withdrew all his customers and directed them to another person who was willing to pay him his share on what comes in through him.

This is a story of a person whom God has blessed with either work or business and refuses to pay or give God's share.

- For those who want to grow in business - pay tithe of income before removing expenses. It's a way of telling God to do more.
- For those who work and are on monthly salary, pay tithe above the salary's tithe. If you desire a higher position in the organization of higher salary, be paying the tithe of the salary or the position you are aiming at.

Let us consider how the Jews were paying their tithes.

Throughout the Bible, there is only on full detail analysis, the Lord Jesus Christ gave the analysis when he was teaching.

Luke 18 v 11 - 12

18:11 ***The Pharisee stood and prayed thus with himself, God, I thank thee, that I am not as other men are, extortioners, unjust, adulterers, or even as this publican.***

18:12 ***I fast twice in the week, I GIVE TITHES OF ALL THAT I POSSESS.***

What I want to bring from here is the way Jesus said this Pharisee pays his tithe; ***"I give tithes of all that I possess".*** Can you boldly say this? So it's not something you just do, it is something to be done accurately with caution. If you want to fully experience the full blessing of Tithe, then find out how to do it properly and do it promptly. If you choose to do it your way, take whatever you get, don't try to prove with your experience that Ministers are just eating your tithe. If you pay your tithe anyhow, how you want it, don't be offended if you don't get the blessing. The problem is never God; the problem is always other factors involved which includes you.

If you want to key into a company that none can fire (sack) you, take the salary (some of it if so desire) put it in an envelope, write at the back "Lord I use this seed to key into this company (write the name)" drop it on the altar not offering bag. There should be no middle person between you and God. But this does not give you the license to misbehave with the confidence that none can fire you, God will.

Kindly Note: Tithe is not a law of the Hebrews - I mean it's not one of the laws God gave to the children of Israel. Tithe has been in existing even before Isaac that gave birth to Jacob who is the father of the Israelites was born. Abraham's name was still Abram when he met Melchizedek, King Salem, whom he paid tithe to, **Genesis 14 vs 18**. So tithe is not among the law Jesus said is abolished. But if you choose not to pay tithe, don't bother to call God on whatever happen to your finance.

Paying of tithe is good. Even if God did not attach blessings to it, it's a good thing.

If we will be honest with ourselves, tithe is the major giving that we do faithfully than every other giving. This helps us to contribute to the growth of the work of the Ministry and at the same time connects our finances to God.

THE BLESSING OF TITHE

Malachi 3 v 10 – 12

3:10 *Bring ye all the tithes into the storehouse, that there may be meat in mine house, and prove me now herewith, saith the LORD of hosts, if I will not open you the windows of heaven, and pour you out a blessing, that there shall not be room enough to receive it.*

3:11 *And I will rebuke the devourer for your sakes, and he shall not destroy the fruits of your ground; neither shall your vine cast her fruit before the time in the field, saith the LORD of hosts.*

3:12 *And all nations shall call you blessed: for ye shall be a delightsome land, saith the LORD of hosts.*

- **Pour you out a blessing that there shall not be room enough to receive it**
- **I will rebuke the devourer for your sakes, and he shall not destroy the fruits of your ground**
- **Neither shall your vine cast her fruit before the time in the field**
- **All nations shall call you blessed**
- **For ye shall be a delightsome land**

Tithe makes God to know if He can trust you or not. Like I said; the tithe you give to God is his own share for bringing money to you. That is partnership and I don't think even you will want to continue doing business with someone who always cheats you in.

"He that is faithful in little shall be faithful in much".

Give God reasons to trust you and to entrust much into your hand by paying or even out paying your tithe regularly. God's blessings will overflow in your life. When you read the same **Malachi 3:10-12** and **Proverbs 3:9-11.** The blessings of God will be pouring to others around you. Everything about you will go well.

The devourer, waster will be rebuked for your sake. There will be no money is not coming or I don't know what I am doing with my money. Sickness will not take money away from you, unnecessary spending will not come your way and there will always be addition.

Tithe brings business ideas from God, undeniable favour; grace beyond explanation people from different places will begin to contact you. Don't forget wisdom is one of the major tool needed for a successful life and business. Your understanding will be open to do something that will uplift you or your business. I am glad, I am not the pastor of your Church neither do I know him in person; else you say I am saying all these because I want to eat your tithe, I am a fellow brother in Christ like you, I pay my tithe also. Listen to me; whether you pay your tithe or not God's work will still be done, only selfish and stingy people argue about tithe, all they search for in the Bible is reasons why they should not pay tithe. Even if I don't get special blessing from God as a result of my tithe, I will still pay tithe as long as am still making money, I have paid tithe for an amount of money I was in need of which did not come in at the time I expected it, instead of allowing anger and frustration to make me upset, I decided I will still do more, finally I got a contract that gave me a profit very close to the amount I have paid tithe for long time ago, I said to God;

"Almost cannot kill a bird, this is not the money I paid tithe for, I will give you tithe of this also and seed from the profit, whenever is convenient, send me my money in full in a day, I don't want it twice".

These are some of the things we do that makes supernatural finance to burst out. By the time all of them accumulates, God will not only send me the money, but will add interest to it to compensate my patience and trust in Him or give me an idea that I can introduce into anything that has to do with money that will change my life forever. What have you tried with tithing? God wants you prosperous; that is why he wants you to pay your tithe. Don't let the idea that it is the ministers that eat it make shy away from it, the devil is trickish, he uses very little things to hold big things, don't worry about who eat it, let it be a transaction between you and God. You can't even trust the prayer of some ministers on your tithe, just trust God, He is faithful.

I have stretch enough on tithe issue. I believe a word is enough for the wise and I am aware that you are a wise child of God who is earnestly and honestly looking for answers to questions that you can apply to your personal life. I am doing my part already by explaining these things to you. Your part is to understand them; believe them and put them to work.

If you really want to enjoy the blessings of tithe, pay tithe for expected amounts, needs that you can't afford with the money with you or property you desire to have, paying tithe this way brings God, the ministry and the minister into action, as I

have said, God's aspect is settled so we will be left with the ministry and the Minister, with this you can tell if you get the blessing of tithe or not. If you don't get it at the time expected, then the minister and the ministry is to be questioned. If you have solid relationship with the Lord, even though it is delayed, your expectation shall not be cut short, God is faithful, he cannot forget your labour of faith, He will make sure you have it somehow or some way so that you can trust him and have faith in him more. He may either grant what you desired or give you supper ideas that will help you to get the amount you paid tithe for. God cannot owe any man and not pay. If the place of the minister and the ministry is intact, your expectation will come at the right time if not earlier than you expected. Behold I show you a more excellent way to pay tithe, know where fault is if the blessing is not received and the assurance of your reward.

Let's see what is next.

THE ROLE OF A MINISTER IN THE RELEASE OF THE BLESSING OF TITHE

The office of a minister cannot be under-estimated when it comes to the release of blessing. Though the giving is to God but the Minister sit in the seat of

Christ as Priest to release God's blessing upon his people. Some Ministers don't know how to release the blessing neither do some know the words of blessing they are to speak upon the person that brings the tithe; some are very good in preaching it and collecting it alone. This is a big limitation to the result that should follow. Tithe will yield to its full capacity if the Minister that received it knows how to release the blessing. If the Minister fails, there is a high chance that you may not receive the blessing at all and if you are paying your tithe with the understanding of the principle of tithing, you may receive the blessing that follows but it can never be in full as it should be if the Minister's contribution is added to it. This is one of the reasons some pay tithe and never experience the blessing. The Minister and Ministry you pay tithe to matters a lot. Many Christians have given up on tithing because they are not experiencing the blessing that follows. We have very little to say about our Ministers, to be on the safer side, learn to relate with the Lord personally, if you will have a solid personal relationship with the Lord, learn the words of the blessing and declare them upon yourself, you will surely experience it. God's word is ever true and never fails.

Whenever you are experiencing the opposite of what the Word says you would, find out from the word of God factors that can affect the expectation.

"The introduction of man in the affairs of God is the limitation of God's power".

"Believe the Word of God, trust it with your life, if it seems to fail you, don't troubleshoot God, troubleshoot every other factor that is or was involved".

THE WORD OF TITHE BLESSING

The words of blessing could be before or after. Before Papa Ab gave tithe to Melchizedek the Prince of Salem had blessed Papa Ab.

Genesis 14 v 18 - 20

14:18 ***And Melchizedek king of Salem brought forth bread and wine: and he was the priest of the most high God.***

14:19 ***And he blessed him, and said, Blessed be Abram of the most high God, possessor of heaven and earth:***

14:20 ***And blessed be the most high God, which hath delivered thine enemies into thy hand.***

And he gave him tithes of all.

"And he blessed him, and said, blessed be Abram of the most high God, possessor of heaven and earth" - This is a word of blessing, a declaration.

"And blessed be the most high God, which hath delivered thine enemies into thy hand" –He acknowledge God in his life

Let's see another one.

Malachi 3 v10-12

3:10 *Bring ye all the tithes into the storehouse, that there may be meat in mine house, and prove me now herewith, saith the LORD of hosts, if I will not open you the windows of heaven, and pour you out a blessing, that there shall not be room enough to receive it.*

3:11 *And I will rebuke the devourer for your sakes, and he shall not destroy the fruits of your ground; neither shall your vine cast her fruit before the time in the field, saith the LORD of hosts.*

3:12 *And all nations shall call you blessed: for ye shall be a delightsome land, saith the LORD of hosts.*

"open you the windows of heaven, and pour you out a blessing that there shall not be room enough to receive it"- This is a word of blessing

"And I will rebuke the devourer for your sakes, and he shall not destroy the fruits of your ground; neither shall your vine cast her fruit before the time in the field"- This is a word of blessing or promise

"And all nations shall call you blessed: for ye shall be a delightsome land" – This is a word of blessing or promise also.

These blessings cannot be fully activated unless the Minister declares them upon you. You know why? They are direct words from God and that makes them resides in the spiritual realm. God is a Spirit if He wants to effect a change on earth, he must make use of a mouth pies. This is the place of a Prophet, Priest, Pastor or Any Minister he place in an office to attend to you. If you pay tithe and these words are not declared upon you, you may not experience the blessing even though you have paid your tithe faithfully. Thank you God bless you is not enough, the blessing must be mentioned in particular.

Declaring these words without power will also make them of none effect. The Minister must release the words from his spirit not his head.
Let me show you an instruction given by God to the Priest of old;
Numbers 6 v 22

6:22 *And the LORD spake unto Moses, saying,*

6:23 *Speak unto Aaron and unto his sons, saying, On this wise ye shall bless the children of Israel, saying unto them,*

6:24 *The LORD bless thee, and keep thee:*

6:25 *The LORD make his face shine upon thee, and be gracious unto thee:*

6:26 *The LORD lift up his countenance upon thee, and give thee peace.*

6:27 *And they shall put my name upon the children of Israel; and I will bless them.*

"On this wise ye shall bless the children of Israel" God specifically told Moses to tell Aaron what to say in particular in prayer upon the Children of Israel, at the end of it the Lord says; "and I will bless them". Why can't God Just bless them without the Priest praying the words upon them?

Same way the promises and blessings of tithes will not just come upon you even though you have paid it without the declaration of the particular words of blessing.

Thanks be unto God, He has made us Kings and Priest, so if your minister fails in this aspect, you can take it up. Offer your tithe directly on the altar of the Almighty God.
We need to clear every hindrance on the blessing of tithe. Be the Prophet of your life, you are a prophet actually if you have received the Holy Ghost, go ahead and be the mouth pies of God to activate the blessing upon your life.

Study the book of Jeremiah, Isaiah, Ezekiel to understand the place of a Man or Prophet in the achievement of God's plan.

FACTORS THAT CAN AFFECT THE BLESSING OF TITHE

1. Robbing God by not paying your tithe at all.
2. Robbing God by paying less than you are supposed to pay.
3. Your attitude towards God because of your tithes.
4. The place of a Minister or a Prophet to declare the Words of blessing.

Note: Whatever you are giving to God, give to Him with due respect and don't try to take honour for something that is your responsibility or trying to hold God to do something for you because of your duties. Paying your tithe or because your tithe is huge is not a reason to raise shoulders to your fellow brothers and sisters not to talk of the ministers. Your humility must increase as God is increasing you. The day you will stumble into the blessing of tithe, that day you will love tithing more than any other financial principles God has laid down.

May the blessing of tithe rest upon you and your household as you practice it in Jesus name. Amen

OFFERING

What is an offering? An offering is an oblation given to a deity. An offering is anything required by a deity. (A spirit being) that we pay homage to. God is a Spirit. Whatever he requires or demands of us, is to be given to Him as an offering. Anything we are giving to God whether he demands it or we are giving Him out of our own wills, it must be offered as an offering. An offering is to be given with reverence, not to be thrown inside the offering bag anyhow or drop on the altar anyhow, or taken anyhow. I am not surprised at this because many people don't have home training both old and young. Many people where brought up in a home where it does not matter how you greet your father, how you give him water to drink or how you hand something over to him, just as many women don't reverence their husband when giving him food or anything, the child learn the same attitude and grow up with it, many grow up with this careless attitude without reverence. This ought not to be so, give to God with reverence, how much is not what count, how much respect you put in it matters more to God.

It is not proper for you to be going to church and begin to be looking for offering everywhere in the house. You had Monday—Saturday to separate your offering. By Sunday morning, you are not supposed to be looking around for your offering. I used to be that way too, Sunday morning is when I will look around to see what is available, out of what I have available, I will take out for offering. I did this until sometimes **2014**. I was in church for Sunday service, when it was time to give offering, the Holy Spirit told me; **"don't bring one hundred naira to me again"**, I was shocked. I thought God is never concerned about the amount. Well that is true to some extent. What you should know is that God expects us to grow. If what you have to give through this month is twenty naira, God expects you to move to fifty naira next month. What you start with is not a problem, being stagnant is what He hates. I said okay Sir. From one hundred naira, I switched to five hundred naira. From here I began to seek a way I can be giving a good offering. I made an envelope, I wrote at the back "**offering**" every day I tried as much as I can to put something in it. I discovered that my offering was more than five hundred that I was paying at the end of the week. On Sunday morning is no longer another day of worrying about offering. All I need is to carry my envelope to church, the same with my tithe.

Now I want you to learn something about this envelope. Any money you put inside cannot be removed by you. You should not make change out of the money under any circumstance. No hunger should make you take money out of it and say I will replace it back. Do not put the money you have separated for offering or tithe in your pocket, because you may mistakenly spend it or forget what money it is. It is a poison that is very dangerous.

So in this light, I'll say to you; always plan your offering. Don't look for a place to buy biscuit because you want small money (change) that you can give for offering. God is not a beggar, grow up. We give the change or little offering not because that is what we have but because we have no regard for offering neither have we come to understand the importance and the blessing on it.

"How much you esteem God is how much he will exalt you".

"How much God means to you, is how much you mean to God"

"How much you respect God is how much people around you will respect you".

"How much you respect and honour God is how much people respect and honour you".

"If you want men to look up to you, you have to learn to look up to God?"

"When you learn to fall on your kneel before God, God will make people to bow to you whether you like it or not".

There are different types of offerings but the major ones are;

FREE WILL OFFERING

Just as it sound, free will offering, is an offering we give willingly out of our own free mind that we choose to give to God. This type of offering may not really have anything attached to it. That is; you are not giving it because of what God did for you or what you want him to do for you. You give it of your own will. Though you are giving it from your own will but don't forget God is a deity, a supreme Spirit being that demands homage whatever type of offering you are giving, give with respect. He reserves the right to accept it or reject it. This is what we give in Church on Sundays and any other gathering in Church.

Free will offering also has its own blessing even though it's done of your own will.

After the destructive forty days and forty nights flood; Noah offered sacrifice to God. God did not ask him to. Let's check it

Genesis 8 vs 20 – 22

8:20 ***And Noah builded an altar unto the LORD; and took of every clean beast, and of every clean fowl, and offered burnt offerings on the altar.***

8:21 ***And the LORD smelled a sweet savour; and the LORD said in his heart, I will not again curse the ground any more for man's sake; for the imagination of man's heart is evil from his youth; neither will I again smite any more every thing living, as I have done.***

8:22 ***While the earth remaineth, seedtime and harvest, and cold and heat, and summer and winter, and day and night shall not cease.***

Can you see that? This was a free will offering. The result of Noah's free will offering is the reason the earth is not destroyed by God because human are still as wicked even more as men were during the days of Noah. Even the rainbow you see is a token of

God's covenant with Noah. Who knows what our free will offering can / could do today?

God also told the children of Israel about it, so that they might receive the blessings that follows; Have you ever find out about what Solomon did that placed him for a life transforming encounter with God? We all know that God gave Solomon wisdom. How did it happen? I'll tell you. Two things made it happen. The first one is David his father; he prepared his heart on what to ask God whenever He shows up. Solomon offered burnt offering onto the Lord to the extent that they could not count. It was after that sacrifice God visited him in the dream where Solomon asked God for wisdom, the sacrifice provoked God.

1 Kings 3 vs 4 – 5

> ***3:4 And the king went to Gibeon to sacrifice there; for that was the great high place: a thousand burnt offerings did Solomon offer upon that altar.***
>
> ***3:5 In Gibeon the LORD appeared to Solomon in a dream by night: and God said, Ask what I shall give thee.***

The free will offering Solomon sacrificed unto the Lord moved God from His throne to visit Solomon at night; that visitation is what made Solomon the richest king that ever lived. Solomon was not rich because he was more righteous than you and me, when you read the complete story of Solomon and how he reigned, you will see many of his mistakes and abominations against God. His offering opened the door of his visitation. I believe we all want God to visits us. This is one of the things that can provoke God to come to you and say ***"Ask me whatever you want and I will do it for you"***. I have confidence in this because I know God is still the same.

Malachi 3 vs 6

"I am the Lord, I change not"

So with our free will offering we can have divine encounter with God. As much as it is good to give God freewill offering, it is also important to give your Minister a free will offering. The offering you drop in the offering box or bag is not for the personal use of the Pastor in charge, but the one you give to him / her directly or buy is for his / her personal use. When you give them such offering, they can pronounce any blessing they desire to bless you with and it will surely work in your life. Let me share a little story with you along this line;

"If you want to receive more than you can ask for from God or a minister, provoke his spirit with a surprising gift".

One day, the spirit of the Lord instructed me to buy a study Bible for my Pastor where I worship then. I did not have the money but I worked toward it. I went to bookshop to know the price and the price was around ten thousand naira (2010-2011). I got this big Bible, took it to the Church. I was aware the Pastor did not have such. I took it to him in his office and gave him the receipt. He asked me "what is it"?, I told him a gift my father asked me to give him. I turned to go out of his office while he was opening it. When he opened it, he was amazed and at the same time provoked in his spirit. He called me back immediately and asked me to kneel down. He prayed for me and utter words I can never forget he said; **"I bless you with the dew of heaven", with many words of blessing he blessed me that day.**

Can see what I mean? I worshiped in that church for years but never heard him say such word. You can scarcely hear a minister say; "I bless you with the dew of heaven". It wasn't just coming from his mouth but his innermost being because his soul is satisfied with something he had longed for. Because of what happened that day, I can bless whomever I want to bless with the dew of heaven and it will surely rest upon the person because I have been blessed with it. The meaning of those words is deep. Because of that offering, not only am I blessed for giving that offering but I have also become a custodian of the dew of heaven.

Learn to give a free will offering.

FIRST FRUIT OFFERING

First Fruit Offering is the very first income you receive at the beginning of the year. This doesn't have to be at the beginning of the year. The first money you realize from a job or business is your first fruit. This first fruit started in the wilderness when God gave the children of Israel laws. God told them anything that open the womb belongs to him also the first fruits of their harvest they should also bring to him.

Exodus 22 vs 29

22:29 Thou shalt not delay to offer the first of thy ripe fruits, and of thy liquors: the firstborn of thy sons shalt thou give unto me.

Now don't misunderstand the last line. It doesn't mean they should offer their sons as sacrifices. The first sons were to be taken to the temple of God to minister unto Him and help in the services of the house of God, by helping the priests accordingly. Later God said they can redeem their sons. Our focus is not on the sons but on the offering (first fruit). I like to always maintain the conversation line. God personally demand for the very first money we earn or make at the beginning of the year or the beginning of the job or business.

Now since first fruit offering is part of the law and according to the New Testament testator, the old law has been abolished. Abolishing the old laws does not mean if we find something of great benefit with no harm, we cannot make use of it. Moreover, the theory of offering has been in existence before the Law.

First fruit offering has a blessing attached to it. Here is something you have to know about God. When He put power or blessing inside a thing, the power or blessing remains even if God says he is not using it again.

For Example:- The Holy mountain of God is still full of power (Mount Horeb) even Mount Sinai. Though the Laws have no glory before God anymore but what He says with the law you can get now without the law of Moses but by the Law of Love given to us by Jesus Christ our Lord. The grace of our Lord Jesus Christ in the New Testament makes it possible for us to enjoy the blessings of God without the Old Laws. Before, the Children of Israel have to keep all the Laws to enjoy the blessings but today, we are enjoying the blessings because we are in Christ and keeping the laws of Christ. We enjoy the blessing without the Law, then it was compulsory, but today, it's by choice.

The word of God is infinite. It's always new as though He just said it now. Though the first fruit issue came with the law, if you act on the law of first fruit, you will get the blessing that follows first fruit. Before you say *"**Since it's not compulsory, I don't need to do it**"* let's see the blessings that follows. Throwing the first fruit away is throwing the blessing that follows; moreover it is to be done once in a year.

Proverbs 3 v 9

3:9 Honour the LORD with thy substance, and with the firstfruits of all thine increase:

3:10 SO SHALL THY BARNS BE FILLED WITH

PLENTY, AND THY PRESSES SHALL BURST OUT WITH NEW WINE.

We all want to have riches in all areas of our lives. In the Bible, when we read something, it's good to find out who made the statement and how he lived. If a prophet was to be saying this, we could say 'He is talking about spiritual things'. The man talking here is the unforgettable king that ever lived on earth whose fame of wealth spreads from east to west and from west to south. His name forevermore is great King Solomon. This king Solomon is still the richest king that ever lived. Now here in **Proverb 3 vs 9-10** he is actually showing us some of his secrets of success, he is telling us if we do this, we will have more. That's why I said who is talking matters and when it comes to riches, wealth, success and money, Solomon is worth listening to. King Solomon was speaking by the inspiration of the Holy Ghost through the gift of wisdom, we all know the wisdom king Solomon had is still available in the Holy Ghost that we received today, wisdom is universal, whatever you find in the Prophets, Psalms, Proverbs, Ecclesiastes and songs of Solomon are universal except indicated, mixed or directly connected with the Law.

Sacrificing your first fruit unto the Lord is more than a religious thing, someone that is not an Israelite back then understood this, used it against Israel God's own people and it worked. I don't want to go in details but I will show you the scripture.

2Kings 3 vs 26 - 27

*3:26 **And when the king of Moab saw that the battle was too sore for him, he took with him seven hundred men that drew swords, to break through even unto the king of Edom: but they could not.***

*3:27 **Then he took his eldest son that should have reigned in his stead, and offered him for a burnt offering upon the wall. And there was great indignation against Israel: and they departed from him, and returned to their own land.***

Note: Who or what he offered the burnt offering to is not the point but the offering he offered which is "his first born" and the result that followed.

The Power of first fruit cannot be under-estimated So I'll say don't throw away the blessing because you think it's not compulsory or the money will be too much for you to give or the care of how you will feed your family. Hey! If you are fired at the end of the month with no salary, will you and your family not survive? One of the principles of riches is ability to give what others cannot give.

"Those who worship money find it difficult to release money".

"When you give out, your arms are open to receive more".

So give it. If you want to experience an uncommon financial favour you have to be able to do uncommon giving that everybody cannot do. For the blessing sake and for the fact that God's business needs the money, it's worth giving.

HOW TO GIVE FIRST FRUIT

If you just got a job, the first salary every year is your first fruit and if you have been in the job, every January salary is your first fruit.

If you are a business man/woman, your January sales is your first fruit. Now if you have staff to pay, you can pay them then what is left is your first fruit. **Kindly note;** you are not supposed to be removing unnecessary expenses that you can do without. If you are strong enough to pay your staff from what you already have as at January sales. It is better you use your personal money and give a completer first

fruit. This is better for you because the more you give, the more you receive.
As for the January tithe, it's okay not to remove it but you can still remove it if you want to, either ways is fine with God. If you have extra money that can cover up for the tithe, you can pay it.

This is becoming annoying! Yeah I know I understand how you feel, because it seems difficult that is why many don't do it, then we can begin to see why we are not all experiencing what the Bible says about us. It seems you have to give everything we have to God hmmm. Do we have another reason why we are living if not to give God all we can lay our hands on? Though it's our responsibility but God is kind enough to bless us for doing what we are made to do. It's like you saying thank you to the spoon you used to eat. We don't do that because we know the reason we bought the spoon is to use it to eat. Yet God says thank you to us for doing what he made us for. God deserves a clap for that. He is a grateful father.

Still under offering!

THANKS GIVING OFFERING

"Those who acknowledge good deeds and appreciate them will surely see more of such deeds".

When we say thanksgiving, we are talking about letting the one we are thanking knows that we acknowledge what He has done, what He is doing and what He is going to do and show appreciation. Thanks giving offering is divided into two forms:-

1. Offering of thanks to God by rending the calves of our lips.
2. Giving an offering (money or something valuable) to God as an act of appreciation of something he has done for us.

I said previously, that freewill offering has no specific thing attached to it. You don't give a freewill offering because of what God has done or what God will do. Thanks giving offering is attached to what God has done specifically. You can give a thanksgiving offering for something you prayed for and have the knowing that you have received it according to your faith that has not manifested in the material world (Physical) or something God has done.

Let's talk about the rendering of the calves of our lips as offering of thanksgiving

RENDERING OF THE CALVES OF OUR LIPS

What does the word says about our giving of thanks. Let search some scripture concerning this:-

Psalm 95 vs 2

95:2 ***Let us come before his presence with thanksgiving, and make a joyful noise unto him with psalms.***

Hebrew 13 Vs 15

13:15 ***By him therefore let us offer the sacrifice of praise to God continually, that is, the fruit of our lips giving thanks to his name.***

"**Our lips**" here is the same as the "calves of our lips" in ***Hosea 14 vs 2.***

From here it is noted that we can give thanks to God with lips, this kind of offering is acceptable by God.

Psalm 50 Vs 14

"Offer unto God thanksgiving; and pay thy vows unto Most High".

1 Thessalonians 5 Vs 18
"In everything give thanks: for this is the will of God in Christ Jesus concerning you".

Jonah 2 v 9
But I will sacrifice unto thee with the voice of thanksgiving; I will pay that that I have vowed. Salvation is of the LORD.

Giving thanks unto the Lord for what He has done is required of us and God delight in the praises of His people. When you are giving thanks, you begin to talk about His goodness, His loving kindness, His power, His love, His mercy, His care and so on, in the middle of this, you'll begin to call Him His majestic names as the Spirit brings words into your mouth. Thanksgiving leads to praise and from praise to magnifying God, as you magnify Him, He is exalted, as you exalt Him, you will be lifted.
God delight in this than anything you could offer Him. Actually this is His sweet incense with sweet odour.

Rendering the calves of our lips is very important, around 2009 - 10, I was used to waking up at midnight just to render the calves of my lips unto the Lord. I will pray a very short prayer like; **"O Lord,**

thank you so much for the love you have for me, thank you for watching over me, am sleeping and enjoying my sleep but you are awake just to make sure am safe. For this I thank you". I say the same thing almost any time I wake up to ease myself at night while my eyes are very heavy of sleep. Just as usual, I did the same thing one night, went back to sleep, in few minutes, while I was still rolling waiting for sleep to carry me to dream land, someone came through the wall, stood very close to me and asked ***"what exactly do you want me to do for you".*** I answered the best way I knew how, immediately I finished talking, he disappeared, I went to sleep thinking it one of the people around that asked me that. After three days, I was in a truck on Marine bridge at Apapa thinking about the words, the voice came to me and asked "**who else in the world could ask you that question?"** immediately my understand was opened and I said dear Lord, I didn't know you're the one, then I replied the question according to my desire and he granted it. I will tell you what I asked that he granted in another book. What I want you to see here is what rendering the calves of our lips could do. Learn it, practice it and do it with consciousness.

GIVING AN OFFERING OF THANKSGIVING

Giving an offering of thanksgiving is also important. It is not complete when God do something great for you and you stay on one part of rendering the calves of your lips. Thanksgiving of rendering the calves of our lips is everyday thing.

Now, know this; Faith is in words and action, Love is in words and demonstration (love has a touch, if you love, you must reach out with the hands of love), appreciation is in words and in action. After giving thanks unto God by rendering the calves of your lips, you step forward by giving an offering (money or valuable item) to Him. Poor mentality says; "**Whatever amount I am giving to God does not matter, after all God does not spend money**". Find out if Jesus ever used money to do anything in His earthly Ministry. If Jesus ever spent money then God does spend money. You know why? Jesus said "**I and my father are one**" in another place He says "**Those things I see my father do always, the same I do**" in another place he said "**my father work hitherto therefore I work**".

I know anyone that speak on this **("whatever amount I am giving to God does not matter after all, God does not spend money")** wise is in the category of those who don't study their Bible, and are raised in Churches where poverty is part of their inheritance in Christ, who see suffering as part of their Christianity.

Let me help you a bit to see if Jesus Christ whom you believer that is if you do, spent money or not.

John 4 v 8

4:8 (For his disciples were gone away unto the city to buy meat.)

The disciples of Jesus Christ left their business to follow him; the Lord Jesus was responsible for their feeding. According to this scripture the disciples went to get food that they will all eat and according to the story, the Lord Jesus was also hungry. Money is what the disciples went with to buy the food.

John 13 v 29

13:29 For some of them thought, because Judas had the bag, that Jesus had said unto him, BUY THOSE THINGS THAT WE HAVE NEED OF AGAINST THE FEAST; or, that he should give something to the poor.

For your information, Judas Iscariot was the one holding the bag of money that they carried along. If Jesus did not need money, he will not have a Treasurer. And here, the Lord gave instruction to

Judas to buy something that they may need out of the money with him. Here again, Jesus Christ spent money. At the mouth of two or three witness a matter is established.

We all know that the disciples left their various occupation to follow Jesus Christ, and the Lord himself left his carpentry occupation for the Work of God, so all the money they had were money given by those who believed in him and in God. Jesus collected offerings and seeds.

So know now that God do spend money. What does He spend it on? God spend money on his business, God's business is saving souls all over the world by spreading the gospel of our Lord Jesus Christ. Take note.

For the man that is ready for exploit who has positioned himself for greatness, I speak on this wise **"I will make your bank account statement drop down for a moment"**. I say for a moment because you cannot out give God. It won't be long you will experience reimbursement. Your joy will increase from one level to another.

Let's consider some people who God did something significant for that came back with thanksgiving. Who either rendered the Calves of their lips or with thanks giving offering.

The story of Hannah the mother of Samuel is a very good example. Hannah prayed to God for a son, God granted her desire. She conceived and bore a son; the name of the son is Samuel who succeeded Eli.

1Samuel 1 vs 24

> ***1:24 And when she had weaned him, she took him up with her, with three bullocks, and one ephah of flour, and a bottle of wine, and brought him unto the house of the LORD in Shiloh: and the child was young.***

This woman went back to the house of God with valuable items. She did not only offer offering of valuable items to God but she also render the calves of her lips.

1 Samuel 2 vs 1

> ***2:1 And Hannah prayed, and said, My heart rejoiceth in the LORD, mine horn is exalted in the LORD: my mouth is enlarged over mine enemies; because I rejoice in thy salvation.***

The kind of prayer the woman offered here is prayer of thanksgiving; you can study the chapter **2 vs 1-11** to know the rest of the story.

What I want you to see is she offered the fruit of her lips and also appreciated God for her son. This also made her conceive more children after Samuel.

Another one is the story of ten lepers whom Jesus cleans and only one of them returned to say thank you. After saying thank you Jesus, Jesus made him whole. **Luke 17 v 12**

Now let me explain that, lepers are people who get attacked by leprosy, little by little it eats the body of the person until the whole body is consumed. When Jesus healed them, the sickness departed. The body part the sickness has eaten is where it stops. Their bodies won't be eaten by the sickness anymore. But the one that returned to give thanks, Jesus made whole; that is; Jesus restored to him every single part of his body that the leprosy had eaten, his skin became normal as though he has never come in contact with leprosy before. This is the difference between being healed and being made whole. When you are made whole, everything you lost as a result of whatever you went through will be restored unto you. Just like the case of Job, God made him completely whole after his afflictions.

If you have an offering give, if you don't have an offering but can work towards it, do so but if you don't have at all or any mean to get, render the calves of your lips whole heartedly, God sees it all. But I will suggest you do both after the Lord has done something great for you.

Luke 17 vs 17- 19

17:17 And Jesus answering said, Were there not ten cleansed? but where are the nine?

17:18 There are not found that returned to give glory to God, save this stranger.

17:19 And he said unto him, Arise, go thy way: thy faith hath made thee whole.

You can read the whole story from the eleventh verse same book. So many people did similar things in thanksgiving. So it is very important (compulsory) to give this unto God. It's for our good. If you have thanksgiving offering, don't boast on it, render it unto the Lord with the rendering of the calves of your lips. In other words, render both, God deserves it all.

PEACE OFFERING

Peace offering is an offering offered for atonement. More like something you give someone that you offended to pacify their anger. It is not bribing the person; it is doing something that will make the person happy after you have done something that made the person sad or angry. This could be in words, works or in giving of gift. It is important to learn when and how to tender an apology, apology or a simple sorry could pacifies anger if tendered at the right time with a honest sense of rumors but I want you to know that sorry does not fix everything even if it is heartfelt, neither is it a currency to pay for what you have destroyed. Sorry is an act of acknowledging you were wrong and you did not mean to cause the damage that has been caused. This does not repair the damage you have caused. When you say sorry, it does not mean the person is automatically healed from all the injuries you have caused. This is why many don't understand why the person they said sorry to is still not happy after they have said sorry. If your sorry did not bring happiness back immediately, you have to proceed to doing whatever you can to make the person happy again. This helps a lot in building all kinds of relationships.

Whatever you have to do to make the person to be happy again is a **Peace Offering**. If you sin against God or someone that caused so many injuries, after acknowledging your faults, proceed to offering a peace offering either by gifts that will make the one you offended happy or by doing things that will make the person happy. You don't just say sorry and then continue as though nothing happened. This is very important in the life of a husband and wife, children and their parents, Church members and their Pastors and Parents, even place of work.

There are some things we do that sorry is not enough to fix it, if peace offering is not given to pacify or avert the punishment, even though the person you have offended has accepted your apology, you will still be punished only that your punishment will be reduced. So also, there are some things we could do to offend people that if we don't acknowledge them, they can bring death. When we acknowledge them, give an offering for them both in gift and in works, we will still be punished, only that the death will be removed. But we will learn a lesson that we will never forget. Be careful how you hurt people, you don't know who is who. Sorry is never enough! This is what King David offered to God when he said; **"I will not give to God that which cost me nothing".** So whatever you are going to give as peace offering must cost you something.

2Samuel 24 v 24 – 25

24:24 ***And the king said unto Araunah, Nay; but I will surely buy it of thee at a price: neither***

will I offer burnt offerings unto the LORD my God of that which doth cost me nothing. So David bought the threshing floor and the oxen for fifty shekels of silver.

24:25 *And David built there an altar unto the LORD, and offered burnt offerings and peace offerings. So the LORD was entreated for the land, and the plague was stayed from Israel.*

Though King David had said sorry to God, but it was not enough, the killing continued. You can read the story from verse 1. The hand of the Angel withdrew while the sacrifice was being offered. So from here, it is clear that saying sorry is never enough when you have caused a severe damage.

- ✓ **Husbands, learn this!**
- ✓ **Wife, practice this!**
- ✓ **Children, build your manners with this!**
- ✓ **Christians, make this a life style!**

If you ever do something that make someone close to you very sad, angry or hurt, after acknowledging with a heart felt sorry, do whatever is within your capacity to bring peace again and make the person happy.

God bless you as you practice this.

PARENT OFFERING & CHARITY

According to the hierarchy, after God, our parent is next. Giving to our parent is not optional, it is compulsory. It doesn't matter how small what we are making is, always make sure you give to your parent. Making them happy make them pray for you. Don't give to them with murmuring and bitterness; give to them happily as you give to God happily, if you don' have as at the time of need, explain to them. Parents are more like deity; they stand in a very high place of spiritual authority. Many lives have been shattered today because of misbehavior to parents that placed a curse on them.

Let me show you a little secret about parental blessing; when your mother and your father prays for you, no being born of a woman can stand against you. Parents are the head of Principalities of mankind. Just as their prayer can save you from dangers planted by whoever is born of a man and a woman they can also be a sure link to destroy their children's lives. Be liberal in your giving; always be willing to give to those that have less around you. When you do that, you are rendering God's service.

God says; "**he that gives to the poor lends to me, I will repay**". Every giving activity you carryout, you are lending to God and God will repay.

Note: For quick and fast result, add evangelism or sponsoring evangelical work.

So far I have listed four major things that anyone who desire to be successful financially in Christ Jesus should apply to their spiritual activities. To be financially successful, it a matter of choice, the choice is not made with mouth alone but your practical application of the principles God has set for such blessings.

I did not mention anything about prayer because prayer is not what makes you rich financially. If it were so, the richest people in the body of Christ would be the prayer warriors. I am a man of prayer and I do believe in prayers. Understanding this kingdom financial principle has nothing to do with how prayerful you are. If you happen to be prayerful, it will help a whole lot, things will happen faster and if there is any delay you can call for re-enforcement. These principles works without prayers, if two people need financial help; and one is only praying and the other told God about it and uses any of these principles, the prayerful one may not receive anything and if he does, it will be something little. The one that applied wisdom will get desired results as fast as possible.

Don't you understand? Prayer will not work when you are to use faith? This is a basic principle from the sovereign God. Many ministers are in lack of finance because of the lack of the knowledge of these principles and yet they are praying heavily and some of those who know them don't know how to apply them.

"Knowledge is not power but the application of knowledge is power -Pastor Chris Oyakhilome.

"You don't know what you know until you are profitable by it" - Bishop David Oyedepo.

What you know is not profitable until you apply it in the area where it's needed. These principles work independently. If you use seed power without offering power, you will still get result and if you use offering power without tithe power, you will still get result. Know this; offering will not make God rebuke the devourer for you neither will tithe provoke God to visit you to ask you what you want him to do for you. Only freewill offering that shakes heaven and move earth will. So be wise in your decisions.

This I say is a matter of choice!

FACTORS THAT CAN AFFECT THE BLESSING OF YOUR OFFERINGS

God Almighty is the father of all, He reserves the right to decide if your offering is acceptable or not. In most cases, when God rejects an offering you may not know except you are the type that have expectation on the offering you are giving to God. From detail study of the scriptures, the following are discovered to be major reasons why an offering may be rejected by God.

1. **Living a disobedient life:-** Living a disobedient life with God makes God lost pleasure in His Children. God is not interested in our offering as much as He is interested in our Heart. God is after us not after ours. Walking in the path of righteousness, living your life according to His Word makes everything or anything you offer to God pleasurable to Him.

   1Samuel 15 v 22 – 23

   15:22 And Samuel said, Hath the LORD as great delight in burnt offerings and sacrifices, as in obeying the voice of the LORD? Behold, to obey is better than sacrifice, and to hearken than the fat of rams.

15:23 ***For rebellion is as the sin of witchcraft, and stubbornness is as iniquity and idolatry. Because thou hast rejected the word of the LORD, he hath also rejected thee from being king.***

Let your life be a reflection of the Word of God, and then shall your offering be pleasant to God.

2. **Disobedient to direct instructions:** Christians are very wonderful when it comes to adhering to instructions from the Holy Spirit concerning giving money to a fellow Christian, Church in need or other giving that involve money. Many Christians are quick in either concluding it is their mind or it's the devil because the devil knows they already had plan for the money. Hahahahaha! Very funny. The devil will never ask you to give money for anything that pertain to God, the day it become possible for the devil to influence people to give for the Glory of Jesus Christ that day he will be re-instated to his formal Angelic position. It is not within him to do good or do anything that will make anyone believe in God. This is my question to such person; before you gave your life to Christ, how many times has your mind told you to give to any Church? You

see, it is not your mind, it is the Holy Ghost and I will advise you never ascribe a thing like that to the devil so that you will not make the deadliest mistake of your life by sinning against the Holy Ghost. This is similar to what the Jews said when the Lord talked about the unforgivable sin. Some won't give the exact amount the Holy Ghost asked them to give, when you disobey this way, whatever you give, may not be accepted. We must always understand that the Holy Ghost is the same as the Almighty God; His instruction must be carried out according to His prescribed order. Those whom He cherishes He instructs to complete the amount, all don't have this second chance.

Hebrews 3 v 15

3:15 While it is said, today if ye will hear his voice, harden not your hearts, as in the provocation.

3. **Blemish offering:-** Offering a blemish offering can put you in the position of not receiving a blessing. God said to the children of Israel that any offering they bring to Him must be without Spot or Blemish. Today, we don't offer offering of

ram and goat, so is it still possible for offering to be blemish? Yes it is possible. Let us look into the possibilities;

i. Offering something that is too below your capacity can dent your offering. God knows our capacity. Giving a hundred naira when God knows your capacity can give five hundred naira as Sunday offering or any need in the House of God is not good for you.

Genesis 4 v 3 - 6

4:3 *And in process of time it came to pass, that Cain brought of the fruit of the ground an offering unto the LORD.*

4:4 *And Abel, he also brought of the firstlings of his flock and of the fat thereof. And the LORD had respect unto Abel and to his offering:*

4:5 *But unto Cain and to his offering he had not respect. And Cain was very wroth, and his countenance fell.*

4:6 *And the LORD said unto Cain, Why art thou wroth? and why is thy countenance fallen?*

4:7 *If thou doest well, shalt thou not be*

> ***accepted? and if thou doest not well, sin lieth at the door. And unto thee shall be his desire, and thou shalt rule over him.***

ii. **Giving money that cannot be spent:-** Many don't care if the money they are giving is spendable or not. This is so because the money they are giving for offering is the change they collected from the taxi driver, the bike rider, change from aboki, change from filling station or any money that they found available at home. This ought not to be so. Prepare your offering; make sure it is spendable money, pray to God for acceptability and place a request on it. The Children of the world buy new notes to spray in parties and clubs. They pay extra for the exchange of their old notes for new notes (mints) so that they will be honorable during the spray of the money. I don't think it is too much if we do even more. It's good to give good things to God. When we say give something good to God, it is not only in quantity, it has so much to do with quality.

iii. **Humility in your giving:** Since I gave my life to Christ till now, I have not seen Christians been trained on how to give an offering to God. I mean attitude of giving offering to God. On several occasions, you see Christians throwing money on the altar or offering bag while standing still like a log of wood without reverence in such a manner you cannot give something to a beggar. Give to God with respect, acknowledging He is there watching you as you give your offering. Don't throw money to offering bags anyhow, drop your offering with reverence. The way I see many throw offering to the altar or offering bag, if something is thrown to me that way, I will not accept it even though I am in need of it. This helped me to understand why many don't get rewarded for the offering they give. Humble yourself before God. Give with respect, give with Joy, give with happiness, give with singing and dancing, and give whole heartedly.

Note: All offerings must be given with expectation, including Sunday service and any other gathering free will offerings. There must be something you request God to do for you as a result of the offering you are giving; this is not really because of the reward but it will consistently help you to know

when your offering is accepted by God and help you to be cautious in your giving. Every offering and giving that God honours always produces a reward and a blessing. Don't give without expectation. Even the instruction offering or giving by the Holy Ghost has its reward.

EXPECT IT!!!!!!!!!!!!!!!!!!!!!!!!!!!!!!!!!!!!!!!

NOTE: The New Testament says very little about offering; Apostle Paul talked about contributions made for him and contributions for the Saints which he says should be done willingly. Old Christians that have stock with these alone has been the reasons the name "Church rat" was introduced as an icon of Christians. In the Book **"Am I a True Christian?"**, and **"How to Know a True Prophet of Jesus Christ"**, I made it clear that the Old Testament doctrines should not be mixed with the New Testament doctrines. Offerings, Seeds and Tithes existed before the Law.

Moreover, there is no need for argument, everything I have written in this Book are not by force and there is no place where it is written that if you don't do them you will go to hell, No. So it's all a matter of Choice.

- Salvation is not by force, it is by choice.
- Receiving the baptism of the Holy Ghost with evidence of speaking in other tongues is a choice not by force.
- Living the Christian life that is; walking in newness of life is by Choice and not by Force
- Being rich and being poor is by choice is not by force.
- Spending eternity in Paradise is by Choice and not by force.
- Living a Holy life is by choice not by force.
- Living by the Principles of the Kingdom of God is not by force, only don't blame God for your miseries

NO NEED FOR ARGUMENT!

- If the ways of riches are easy, everybody will be rich.
- If everybody is rich, who will be the poor?
- If everybody is wise, who will be the foolish?
- If everybody is a leader who will be the follower?
- If everybody is a master, who will be the servant?
- If everybody is the head, who will be the tail?
- If everybody is CEO who will be the staff and the factory worker?

- Life and death is a choice, choose wisely.

Being poor and wretched on earth may not stop you from entering heaven, that is if you are able to endure till the end, but you may still be a messenger in Paradise just like the poor Lazarus.

Mark my word, the economy of every nation under heaven is going to grow worse, frustration will cause many to fall away, and God is trying to protect you from frustrations that will arise as a result of lack of money which will make many Christians to fall away.
DON'T BE A VICTIM!

Note: God does not bless you because you do all or any of these, you are already a blessed person since the day you came to Christ, and all these will only help you to experience increase and the manifestation of the blessing of God in your life. You can be a blessed person and live a poor life.

Before you start tangible and dangerous giving, make sure you have tried and trusted the Minister or the Ministry to avoid frustrations.

OTHER THINGS YOU SHOULD ALSO DO TO LIVE A PROSPEROUS LIFE

- Praying for the peace of Jerusalem and the Church of Jesus Christ–

  Psalm 122 v 6 -9

122:6 ***Pray for the peace of Jerusalem: they shall prosper that love thee.***

122:7 ***Peace be within thy walls, and prosperity within thy palaces.***

122:8 ***For my brethren and companions' sakes, I will now say, Peace be within thee.***

122:9 ***Because of the house of the LORD our God I will seek thy good.***

- Preaching the Gospel or sponsoring evangelical works.

  Psalm 35 v 27 - 28

35:27 ***Let them shout for joy, and be glad, that favour my righteous cause: yea, let them say continually, Let the LORD be magnified, which hath pleasure in the prosperity of his servant.***

35:28 *And my tongue shall speak of thy righteousness and of thy praise all the day long.*

And also;

Matthew 6 v 33

6:33 *But seek ye first the kingdom of God, and his righteousness; and all these things shall be added unto you.*

- **Living the Christian life**

Psalm 1 v 1 – 6

1:1 *Blessed is the man that walketh not in the counsel of the ungodly, nor standeth in the way of sinners, nor sitteth in the seat of the scornful.*

1:2 *But his delight is in the law of the LORD; and in his law doth he meditate day and night.*

1:3 *And he shall be like a tree planted by the rivers of water, that bringeth forth his fruit in his season; his leaf also shall not wither; and whatsoever he doeth shall prosper.*

1:4 *The ungodly are not so: but are like the chaff*

which the wind driveth away.

1:5 *Therefore the ungodly shall not stand in the judgment, nor sinners in the congregation of the righteous.*

1:6 *For the LORD knoweth the way of the righteous: but the way of the ungodly shall perish.*

- **Believing your Minister, honouring him and doing according to his instruction.**

2Chronicles 20 v 20

20:20 *And they rose early in the morning, and went forth into the wilderness of Tekoa: and as they went forth, Jehoshaphat stood and said, Hear me, O Judah, and ye inhabitants of Jerusalem; Believe in the LORD your God, so shall ye be established; believe his prophets, so shall ye prosper.*

- **Keep your mouth from speaking evil against fellow Christians and Ministers and all kinds of evil speaking that is not consistent with the Gospel. Live a life free of murmuring, continue**

giving of praise and honor to the Lord in all your endeavors.

Proverbs 12 v 14

12:14 *A man shall be satisfied with good by the fruit of his mouth: and the recompense of a man's hands shall be rendered unto him.*

Proverbs 18 v 20 - 21

18:20 *A man's belly shall be satisfied with the fruit of his mouth; and with the increase of his lips shall he be filled.*

18:21 *Death and life are in the power of the tongue: and they that love it shall eat the fruit thereof.*

Also,

1Peter 3 v 10 – 12

3:10 *For he that will love life, and see good days, let him refrain his tongue from evil, and his lips that they speak no guile:*

3:11 *Let him eschew evil, and do good; let him seek peace, and ensue it.*

3:12 *For the eyes of the Lord are over the*

righteous, and his ears are open unto their prayers: but the face of the Lord is against them that do evil.

Attaining to this level will position us for Wealth Transfer.

Brotherly love in the house of God and in our daily life matters;

Ephesians 4 v 31 – 32

4:31 *Let all bitterness, and wrath, and anger, and clamour, and evil speaking, be put away from you, with all malice:*

4:32 *And be ye kind one to another, tenderhearted, forgiving one another, even as God for Christ's sake hath forgiven you.*

Colossians 3 v 8 – 10

3:8 *But now ye also put off all these; anger, wrath, malice, blasphemy, filthy communication out of your mouth.*

3:9 *Lie not one to another, seeing that ye have put off the old man with his deeds;*

3:10 *And have put on the new man, which is*

renewed in knowledge after the image of him that created him:

1Peter 2 v 1 – 2

2:1 *Wherefore laying aside all malice, and all guile, and hypocrisies, and envies, and all evil speakings,*

2:2 *As newborn babes, desire the sincere milk of the word, that ye may grow thereby:*

After you have mastered these things, then move on to "SECRETS OF WEALTH".

Do you now see why many Children of God are not experiencing the blessing of God? We have not talked about pray yet, by the time you find out the kind of prayers involved in financial prosperity, you will understand what we means when we say "Christianity is not a Child's play", anyone can shout and cry till tomorrow, if you don't do what is to be done, you will live your life as a poor person. Just like a slave.

Psalm 82 v 5 – 7

82:5 *They know not, neither will they understand; they walk on in darkness: all the foundations of the earth are out of course.*

82:6 *I have said, Ye are gods; and all of you are children of the most High.*

82:7 *But ye shall die like men, and fall like one of the princes.*

- **Pray for the peace of your country: This is an instruction that many neglect, but as for you that is ready to live a prosperous life in Christ, you must learn to pray for the peace of your Country and speak no evil about the leaders.**

Jeremiah 29 v 7

29:7 *And seek the peace of the city whither I have caused you to be carried away captives, and pray unto the LORD for it: for in the peace thereof shall ye have peace.*

1Timothy 2 v 1 – 4

2:1 *I exhort therefore, that, first of all, supplications, prayers, intercessions, and giving of thanks, be made for all men;*

2:2 *For kings, and for all that are in authority;*

that we may lead a quiet and peaceable life in all godliness and honesty.

2:3 *For this is good and acceptable in the sight of God our Saviour;*

2:4 *Who will have all men to be saved, and to come unto the knowledge of the truth.*

Romans 13 v 1 – 7

13:1 *Let every soul be subject unto the higher powers. For there is no power but of God: the powers that be are ordained of God.*

13:2 *Whosoever therefore resisteth the power, resisteth the ordinance of God: and they that resist shall receive to themselves damnation.*

13:3 *For rulers are not a terror to good works, but to the evil. Wilt thou then not be afraid of the power? do that which is good, and thou shalt have praise of the same:*

13:4 *For he is the minister of God to thee for good. But if thou do that which is evil, be afraid; for he beareth not the sword in vain: for he is the minister of God, a revenger to execute wrath upon him that doeth evil.*

13:5 *Wherefore ye must needs be subject, not only for wrath, but also for conscience sake.*

13:6 *For for this cause pay ye tribute also: for they are God's ministers, attending continually upon this very thing.*

13:7 *Render therefore to all their dues: tribute to whom tribute is due; custom to whom custom; fear to whom fear; honour to whom honour.*

I suggest you study this book of Romans 13 in The Living Bible. It will give a clear understanding. I have explained it in the book titled "Am I a True Christina?"

Speaking against the government is not good for a Christian that is ready to live a prosperous life.

It is obvious that every man get what he deserves according to the works of His hands

Jeremiah 17 v 5 – 10

17:5 *Thus saith the LORD; Cursed be the man that trusteth in man, and maketh flesh his arm, and whose heart departeth from the LORD.*

17:6 For he shall be like the heath in the desert, and shall not see when good cometh; but shall inhabit the parched places in the wilderness, in a salt land and not inhabited.

17:7 Blessed is the man that trusteth in the LORD, and whose hope the LORD is.

17:8 For he shall be as a tree planted by the waters, and that spreadeth out her roots by the river, and shall not see when heat cometh, but her leaf shall be green; and shall not be careful in the year of drought, neither shall cease from yielding fruit.

17:9 The heart is deceitful above all things, and desperately wicked: who can know it?

17:10 I THE LORD SEARCH THE HEART, I TRY THE REINS, EVEN TO GIVE EVERY MAN ACCORDING TO HIS WAYS, AND ACCORDING TO THE FRUIT OF HIS DOINGS.

- Houour your Minister or any Spiritual leader you are under:- So much blessing lies in the mouth of a Minister. As it is a dangerous thing to disrespect them, so also it is a blessing to respect and Honour them.

They are to be esteemed highly;
1Timothy 5 v 17

5:17 ***Let the elders that rule well be counted worthy of double honour, especially they who labour in the word and doctrine.***

Though it is our responsibility to honour them and yet God blesses us for it if we do it well.

1Thessalonians 5 v 12 – 13

5:12 *And we beseech you, brethren, to know them which labour among you, and are over you in the Lord, and admonish you;*

5:13 *And to esteem them very highly in love for their work's sake. And be at peace among yourselves.*

They are to be esteemed highly both in words and in deeds. When this is done rightly, you will notice prosperity in your life.

Note: Whatever your life is today, it is what you deserve, if you like, argue; God says so. If you want to see a better life, change your ways of life and apply new things. As much as there are Ministers

and Ministries that knows how to preach and collect tithe, seeds and offerings without knowing or concerned whether you get the blessing that should follow or not so also there Ministers and Ministries that knows how to preach it, collect and knows how to rain the blessing of every financial giving you do in the House of God. Find them for your financial increase and stop murmuring.

I should have stop here but it's not complete if I omit the importance of meditation, power of positive thinking and saying the right words.

GOD BLESS YOU.

MEDITATION, POWER OF POSITIVE THINKING AND TALKING

These three principles are very important in our daily lives.

MEDITATION

Meditation simply means recitation of words in your mouth. The English translation express it as quiet talking to one's self, the old English uses the word soliloquizing. It's often compared with attitude of a lunatic, who mutter words; we see the lips moving but the words coming out are more like whispers. The original Hebrew word means to think about, to ponder, mutter and roar so as to attain a spiritual height.

When you meditate, so many things happen –

Let's see 1Timothy 4 vs 15

Meditate upon these things; give thyself wholly to them; that thy profiting may appear to all.

The meditation we see in Joshua 1 vs 8 is the same here. When you meditate, whatever it is you are meditating on will appear for people around you to see. Do you mean I will become what I am meditating on? Yes what you meditate on is who you will become, that is what the scripture says, and that is what I am saying too. Decide on what you want to become and keep saying it.

Psalms 77 v 11 - 12

> ***77:11 I will remember the works of the LORD: surely I will remember thy wonders of old.***
>
> ***77:12 I will meditate also of all thy work, and talk of thy doings.***

Meditate upon the word and the works of God, make a harmonious melody in your heart unto the Lord all day long. Meditation helps your mind to be focused on what you are meditating on, once your mind is in consent with your spirit, your body will cooperate, this will help you achieve what you are aiming at, once your trinity agrees, you shall have whatsoever it is you focus on, keep your mind focused on Jesus the author and the finisher of your faith through meditation.

Aside becoming what you are meditating on, there is something more. When you meditate on the word of

God, you will eventually be fulfilling the basic requirement God demands from us, his children, Jesus says; seek ye first the kingdom of God and his righteousness and everything will be added to you. When you meditate, you will be fulfilling the scripture and the blessing that follows will be added to you. To know more about what to meditate on and how to take advantage of meditation, I recommend you take a personal study on the New Testament portion of the Bible, to know what Jesus says about us and the Apostles, then take a stand and affirm that you are who the Word says you are.
The finalization of this is, you meditate on the word of God by consistently thinking, muttering and saying aloud to yourself what the Word says about you again and again with confidence and boldness as other hears you.

POWER OF POSITIVE THINKING

What are thoughts? Thoughts are like ideas thrown to you by God, Satan, man, your environment or the circumstances around you that you embrace. That is, what you see, feel and hear. These form an envelope of thoughts. When these thoughts have come to maturity, they are manifested through you or for you. In other word, whatever you have as a thought will come to reality if you ponder on it long enough; either positive or negative, when thoughts have come to maturity they begin to materialize, once it starts materializing, nothing can stop it except divine intervention of the Almighty. And for the creator of heaven and earth to be able to deliver you from the power of your thoughts, he will need to redirect your thinking process first. Once your way of thinking is changed, there will be a sudden change in that particular situation.

"The mind has a magnetic force that attracts to you all you think about, whether good or bad" - Pastor Chris Oyakhilome.

The Bible says ***"as a man thinketh in his heart so is he"***.

What you think consistently will surely surface in your life. So guard your heart; for out of it are the issues of life.

Every Child of God is supposed to think like God. A Child is supposed to have the same mind set with his / her father. I know them of old said "**God's ways are not man's ways**" but he did not say God's ways are not his children's ways. The man talking about there is not the one that is in Christ Jesus.

Jesus brought us to God so that we might know his ways.

1Corinthians 2 v 16

> 2:16 ***For who hath known the mind of the Lord, that he may instruct him? BUT WE HAVE THE MIND OF CHRIST.***

Anyone in Christ has the mind of Christ therefore we know the mind of God concerning us and situations, you say how? Through the word of God and his Spirit that dwells in us. So we can think like God. What kind of thoughts are God's thoughts concerning our finance? I will show you some; make sure you make them your thoughts.

Firstly, it is written that Gods thoughts towards us are thoughts of good and not of evil and to take us to an expected end.

Jeremiah 29 v 11 - 13

> 29:11 ***For I know the thoughts that I think toward you, saith the LORD, thoughts of peace, and not of evil, to give you an expected end.***
>
> 29:12 ***Then shall ye call upon me, and ye shall go and pray unto me, and I will hearken unto you.***

> **29:13** ***And ye shall seek me, and find me, when ye shall search for me with all your heart.***

You have to pick this up as your way of thinking, knowing fully well that God's thoughts towards you is for you to prosper and live a good and comfortable life.

Secondly; it is written in ***3 john 1 v 2***

> **1:2** ***Beloved, I wish above all things that thou mayest prosper and be in health, even as thy soul prospereth.***

This also tells you it is God's desire that your business grows, that you receive double promotion and favour in all areas of your life.

Thirdly; it is written **"I give unto you power to make wealth" Deut 8 v 18.** God wants us wealthy so he gives us power to make wealth.

Now that we know the thoughts of God towards us, what should we have in our hearts to be thinking of?

- **Think ownership**; think of buying houses not renting, think of possessing properties all around the world.

- **Think of giving**; the giver is higher than the receiver, and it's more of a blessing to give than

to receive. Also givers never lack because **"God is a giver, so he will make provision for givers to do his business" - Bishop David Oyedepo**.
If you were the type that always look up to the government, family, friends or neighbours, stop it immediately and start thinking of what you can give to others.

- **Think of lending to others**; as it is written **"the borrower is subject to the lender"**. And God has made you the head and not the tail. ***"The LORD shall open unto thee his good treasure, the heaven to give the rain unto thy land in his season, and to bless all the work of thine hand: and thou shalt lend unto many nations, and thou shalt not borrow - Deut. 28 v 12.*** So no more borrowing, you start lending to people. Some will pay back, some won't.

- **Think of yourself as a rich person**; Remember as you think in your heart so are you and it is written **"the rich ruleth over the poor"**. So you are the rich that is ruling but not with wicked ruling like the people of the world who oppresses the poor with their riches. You bless and help the poor with your riches. If there is anything of this nature think on them.

POWER OF TALKING

Talking is speaking out what is in your heart, **"out of the abundance of the heart, the mouth speaks".** Can you see where thoughts and words meet? What you have in your heart is not heard in the physical until you voice it out. When you voice it out, you establish what you have being thinking about. What you are thinking about, what you say, gives what you will see in life. The arithmetic is simple;

Meditation= thought when thoughts are mature, the mouth speak them out which = reality of your life.

"Meditation + thoughts + your words = what happens in your life".

The dangerous part of this is no matter how long it has been, when these begins to work, even you cannot stop it; just as you cannot change a male child to a female after giving birth to him.

Now that you know that what you meditates on forms your thoughts, I believe if your thoughts have been conflicting with God's thoughts for you, you will want to change them. Change your thought by

exchanging the old thoughts you have with God's thought. This process is called renewing your mind.
Once you change what you meditate on, that is, what you say about yourself every day, your thinking will begin to change to the new things you are saying, this means your life will be taking a new and brighter form.

Give attention to the word of God, study it, listen to it an act accordingly. Refuse to pay attention to the wrong news; they will pollute your heart. Don't forget God says we should guard our hearts. Why? So that it will not be polluted, by what? By the things we feel, hear and see. Thoughts are majorly formed through what we feel, hear and see, and what our mouth will say will be materialized.

The power of life and death lies in the power of the tongue. Speak life so that you may live and enjoy riches in every area of your life.

For more understanding on meditation, thought and confession get our book titled **"YOU MUST BE BORN AGAIN"** it is free. You can also place your order for **"HOW A CHRISTIAN SHOULD TALK"** this books explains in detail, how a Christian should think, talk and act.

If you will apply these principles of financial success in the kingdom of God to your daily life, you shall

never be unfruitful or barren and whatsoever you do, you shall surely prosper.
Go, put what you have learnt to work, as you do, the Spirit of the Lord will unveil more secrets to you.

To him that have, more shall be given. Since you already know some now, more shall be given to you. You have to act immediately, if you relent, the devil will steal the words away from your heart. The fact that you have studied this book does not mean the blessing of the principles will work for you automatically. It is not the reader or hearer that is blessed; it is the doer of the works. Faith is action. If you believe what I have shown you, then act accordingly.

I am not a pastor as suppose neither am I saying bring the money to our church. I am one of the sons of God who don't joke with the words of God. I study to show myself approved. All I have been sharing with you is little scratch of what the Holy Spirit has deposited in my heart. Though some he is giving me directly as am writing, whether directly or not they are passing through me therefore they are retained.

As I learn, I increase. I practice them as well and I am still practicing them. This book will not contain testimony if I start showing some of the tremendous result I had shared. All I want you to know is these things worked then, they work today and they will work till Jesus come.

God bless you as you get them to work. Even If I share a thousand testimonies, who will not believe will not believe. Go try them, you will have your own testimonies.

The only prayer I can recommend now is for you to pray unto the Lord of harvest to help you recognize a fertile ground, seeds to sow and bread to eat so that you will have the opportunity to invest into your future and not be hungry while you are doing that.

WORDS OF ADVICE

1. Learn to pray the prayer of worship, praise and thanksgiving.
2. Learn not to worry. Cast your cares upon him. In all things - give thanks.
3. Trust God with your whole heart – Trust in God comes as you fellowship with his word and His Spirit.
4. No matter what happen, say the right words always.
5. Be happy about God always and let the things that matters to God be your focus.
6. Stop the prayer of "God give me" always. Thank Him. He knows your needs .

OUR VISION

To fill the earth with the glory of the knowledge of God, the glory of the knowledge of Jesus Christ and the glory of the knowledge of the Holy Spirit.

"For the earth shall be filled with the knowledge of the glory of the LORD, as the waters cover the sea". Habakkuk 2 v 14

"And this gospel of the kingdom shall be preached in all the world for a witness unto all nations; and then shall the end come". Matthew 24 v 14

OUR MISSION

To deliver the Word of His Grace which is able to build up whosoever believes in Jesus Christ unto a perfect man, unto the measure of the stature of the fullness of Christ. **Ephesians 4 v 13**

Acts 20 v 32

And now, brethren, I commend you to God, and to the word of his grace, which is able to build you up, and to give you an inheritance among all them which are sanctified.

OUR WORKS

We are joining our way to the top, the grace available for us as at now, is what we are utilizing; your support and sponsorship in any form is welcome.

We are fully involved in Evangelical Work; Field Evangelism, Church Evangelism (**personal or combine with other Ministries on request),** free Bible distribution, free Christian books distribution, Free Christian books library as we are working toward a charitable foundation for the less privilege children.

The Lord is doing great things with us these last days. If you want to be a part of us, kindly contact us, if there is any area you can contribute value, potential, intelligence, growth e.t.c kindly let us know.

D. WORD OF HIS GRACE OUTREACH MINISTRY

...the perfection of beauty, the Lord Jesus has shine forth.

For your testimony, Prayer Counseling and sponsorship you can write; E-mail: samfemi1958@gmail.com or call: +2348099712477

BOOKS FROM THIS PEN OF A READY WRITER

1. **You must be born again**
2. **How a Christian should talk**
3. **Secrets of wealth**
4. **How to be a financially successful Christian**
5. **The new creature**
6. **Christ the seed of Abraham**
7. **Christian Growth 1 (for new born to maturity)**
8. **Christian Growth 2 (for the mature to aged)**
9. **Christian Growth 3 (for the aged till departure)**
10. **The man Jesus and the Glorified Jesus**
11. **How to know a true prophet of Jesus Christ**
12. **Am I a true Christian?**
13. **The saved Christians and the Glorified Christians**
14. **The kind of prayers God expects from a Christian**
15. **The Gospel according to Apostle Paul**
16. **The Anti-Christ - Biggest Enemy of Christ**
17. **How to raise a Godly child**
18. **Why should I go to Church?**
19. **How to see what God wants you to see**
20. **Secrets of Supernatural power**

Christian
Growth
1
New Born To Maturity
SAM O. OLUWAFEMI

AM
I
A TRUE
CHRISTIAN
?
SAM O. OLUWAFEMI

HOW
TO KNOW
A TRUE PROPHET
OF JESUS CHRIST
SAM O. OLUWAFEMI

Christ
The Seed
of
Abraham
"Understanding your connection to Abrahamic blessing"
SAM O. OLUWAFEMI

SECRETS
OF
WEALTH
SAM O. OLUWAFEMI

YOU
MUST BE
BORN AGAIN
it is free
SAM O. OLUWAFEMI

www.ingramcontent.com/pod-product-compliance
Lightning Source LLC
LaVergne TN
LVHW010058170826
845678LV00012B/2167

* 9 7 8 9 7 8 5 8 3 2 7 4 7 *